Library of
Davidson College

STUDIES IN HISTORY, ECONOMICS AND
PUBLIC LAW

Edited by the
FACULTY OF POLITICAL SCIENCE
OF COLUMBIA UNIVERSITY

NUMBER 528

A CONSTITUTIONAL HISTORY OF GEORGIA

BY

ETHEL KIME WARE

# A CONSTITUTIONAL HISTORY
OF GEORGIA

BY
ETHEL K. WARE

AMS PRESS, INC.
NEW YORK
1967

Copyright 1947, Columbia University Press
New York

Reprinted 1967
with permission of Columbia University Press

AMS PRESS, INC.
New York, N.Y. 10003

Manufactured in the United States of America

To

MY SISTER
EMMA LOUISE WARE

## ACKNOWLEDGMENTS

IN presenting this *Constitutional History of Georgia,* I should like to make grateful acknowledgment, for material used, to all the authors whose names appear in the bibliography, and to the staffs of the Columbia University Libraries, The New York Historical Society, the Library of Congress, and the Archives of the State of Georgia, for their gracious assistance.

The friends who helped are too numerous to mention, but I take this opportunity to thank, especially, Miss Mary A. Reilly and Miss Virginia Ackerley for their many kindnesses. I wish to express appreciation, also, to Miss Margaret Ladd Franklin, for her timely and generous editorial assistance.

To several members of the Columbia University faculty I am deeply indebted—in particular, to Professor Henry Steele Commager for a stimulating seminar in judicial review and for helpful criticism of the manuscript; and to Professor Allan Nevins whose constant and generous encouragement I cannot acknowledge in mere words here.

The book was written in the knowledge of the whole-hearted support of my sister and brothers and with a warm memory of my mother and father who loved Georgia.

ETHEL KIME WARE

NEW YORK, MAY 1946.

# TABLE OF CONTENTS

|  | PAGE |
|---|---|
| **CHAPTER I** | |
| Pre-Revolutionary Georgia | 11 |
| **CHAPTER II** | |
| The Framing of the First State Constitution | 29 |
| **CHAPTER III** | |
| Learning by Trial and Error | 34 |
| **CHAPTER IV** | |
| Georgia From 1777 to 1789 | 49 |
| **CHAPTER V** | |
| The Framing and Provisions of the Second Constitution | 62 |
| **CHAPTER VI** | |
| Georgia From 1789 to 1798 | 71 |
| **CHAPTER VII** | |
| How the Constitution of 1798 Was Constructed | 77 |
| **CHAPTER VIII** | |
| The Constitution of 1798 in Action | 91 |
| **CHAPTER IX** | |
| Georgia From 1798 to 1861 | 107 |
| **CHAPTER X** | |
| The Convention of 1861—Secession and Constitution | 114 |
| **CHAPTER XI** | |
| The Constitution of 1861 | 122 |
| **CHAPTER XII** | |
| The Constitution of 1865 | 127 |
| **CHAPTER XIII** | |
| The Reconstruction Constitution | 135 |
| **CHAPTER XIV** | |
| Reconstruction | 148 |

## CHAPTER XV
The Convention of 1877 .................................................. 159

## CHAPTER XVI
The Constitution of 1877 ................................................ 168

## CHAPTER XVII
Amendments and Statutes 1877-1945 ............................. 174

## CHAPTER XVIII
Georgia From 1877 to 1945 ............................................ 183

## CHAPTER XIX
The Constitutional Commission of 1945 and Its Work ........ 186

## CHAPTER XX
Conclusions .................................................................. 193

BIBLIOGRAPHY ................................................................ 199

INDEX ............................................................................ 207

# CHAPTER I
# PRE-REVOLUTIONARY GEORGIA

GEORGIA, the youngest of the English colonies, founded as a trusteeship, was converted into a royal colony as the eighteenth century passed its mid-mark. Years before its establishment, the other colonies had bickered and quarrelled with England over Navigation and Trade Acts, and had fought for and won such rights as that of representative assembly. Many other differences of opinion reached the ears and minds of Georgians. Though Great Britain made a strong paternalistic effort to keep it protected and dependent, the young colony mildly resented the Stamp Act and slowly emerged at last to take its place with the sister colonies in open revolt. Today the " Empire State of the South," Georgia gave at first but faint promise of vast unfulfilled possibilities.

Along the Atlantic seacoast from the Savannah River to the St. Mary's lay a row of twelve little settlements, piously named for the saints of the Anglican Church from Saint Paul to Saint Mary. As time passed, they daringly spread up the four main rivers into the interior. When in 1752 the trustees gave over the colony to the Crown, it contained some 2,381 whites and 1,066 Negroes. By 1766 the population had grown to 19,500, by 1772 to 33,000.[1] Few people lived below the Altamaha, but above it were several thriving centers, Savannah, Sunbury, and Augusta, Darien, New Inverness and Midway. Savannah, the oldest city, was a mere village by present standards, with scarcely more than three of four hundred houses, mostly of wood;[2] but it was the center of culture and, in effect, the capital. Here sat the governor, here resided the officials of the royal government. The legislature gathered here in a large two-story building (originally used for the cocoons when a silk industry was expected to develop), the Assembly gather-

[1] A. Johnson, *Georgia as Colony and State*, p. 114.
[2] C. C. Jones, *History of Georgia*, II, p. 21.

ing downstairs and the Council upstairs.[3] Governor Wright had a town house, though, since the removal of restrictions on landholding and slave-holding which had been in effect, he had become one of the big plantation owners, with eleven plantations of from three hundred to six thousand acres each, scattered over the colony. Here, too, lived prosperous merchants like James Habersham, who had also become a plantation owner, deriving two thousand pounds yearly from his acres.[4] Rice was the source of income for these gentlemen, not cotton or silk. The filature at Savannah had burned down in 1758 and since Parliament had given up the idea that Georgia might be a great silk-producing center and had withdrawn its bounty, interest in silk had waned. Habersham, like others, ordered his clothes from London.

Social distinctions were more to be noted in the cities than elsewhere, particularly in Savannah, which was filled with crown officials or with wealthy local spokesmen in the Assembly. English tradition was prevalent here, mixed with Scotch and German. Gentlemen looked after their plantations, engaged in some amusements of the day, (card playing, dueling, horse racing, interludes), and were well read on political, philosophical and religious subjects, if one may judge by the advertisements, published in the *Georgia Gazette,* by the booksellers of the day, who ordered the works of Voltaire, Locke, and Rousseau.[5] Other citizens went about their business of making a living, some professional men, and some business men and merchants, some mechanics and artisans.

About 1745 there had moved into St. John's parish from the Dorchester settlement in South Carolina a group of devout, intelligent New England Congregationalists.[6] Settling in a town

[3] *Colonial Records Georgia* XIII, 7, 309-311; XIV 258, 358, 363, XVIII 46ff.

[4] Johnson, *op. cit.,* p. 117.

[5] A. E. Saye, *New Viewpoints in Georgia History,* p. 137.

[6] G. G. Smith, *Story of Georgia and Georgia People,* pp. 66-67.

which they named Midway, these sturdy hard-working people cleared the swamps and by sheer devotion and hard labor made their section comfortable and prosperous. Lyman Hall, Connecticut-born, joined the group before it moved to Georgia, and acquired two of the choice lots. Other leaders of Georgia prospered here in a spirit of self-reliance and independence. One, for example, was Button Gwinnett, who made his home on St. Catherine's Island to be near his friends Lyman Hall, Benjamin Andrew and Nathan Brownson. Needing a market for their wares, the Midway group decided to have a port of their own, for which they chose a high bluff twelve miles from the ocean up the Savannah River. This port became the little village of Sunbury; it had between eight hundred and a thousand inhabitants—merchants and their families.

Augusta, farther up, became the center of the Indian trade. Inland, but still within the tidewater belt, were Darien, primarily a settlement of rice planters,[7] and New Inverness, in which prosperous Scotch stock-raisers predominated.

Though the Anglican Church was established, its members were out-numbered by the dissenters. Georgia was tolerant to all—from the beginning, Jews, Catholics, Salzburgers and Quakers were welcomed but the legislation of the day showed a distinct Puritan strain. Compulsory church attendance was demanded, work or play on the Sabbath banned, taverns were closed on Sunday, and constables patrolled the streets.[8] There was some interest in charity, little in education except such as was given through tutors and through a sojourn of the sons in England. Much thought was given to the regulations for the slaves, whose numbers were rapidly increasing. Patrols had to be established to keep safety and order, and codes had to be made to protect the slaves' rights, including their right to in-

---

[7] A. M. Schlesinger, *The Colonial Merchants and the American Revolution*, p. 33, called Georgia backward agriculturally as compared with South Carolina. Rice was the staple in the eighteenth century. Indigo was stimulated by parliamentary bounties.

[8] A. Nevins, *The American States During and After The Revolution*, p. 440.

struction, which was favored by such men as James Habersham.

Up-country, along the frontiers of the seaboard settlements, great tides of movement were stirring. The plantation system made it possible for the wealthy man to buy out the small farmer with his fifty to five hundred acres. Some of these displaced farmers settled in the Piedmont regions as the Indians removed from that section. Here might be found the Irish colony of Louisville, the Quakers of Wrightboro, and an influx from Maryland, Virginia and North Carolina, mostly stock raisers with few slaves.[9] Moving farther out was a growing stream of rough, uneducated, but individualistic descendants of indentured servants, pouring in along the back country routes, in flight from the crowding tidewater civilization of older colonies. It was this group which Chief Justice Anthony Stokes described as " crackers " as they swarmed in, taking advantage of liberal head-right laws passed during the Revolution.[10] Of mixed stock, " vigorous, lawless, hard drinkers and dirty fighters " they did not take a lead in the events prior to the Revolution, but they fought in the war and took part in the postwar reconstruction.[11]

It is at the low country and coastal plain settlements that we must look for the beginnings of the story of the struggle for constitutional rights in Georgia. At first their temper was on the conservative side. Because of their scattered locations, the danger of Spanish or Indian attacks,[12] and the large influence of the few prospering commercial centers, any movement of protest or discontent was temporarily smothered. Georgia was not living under a charter, as in the beginning, but under the commission given to the royal governors and the will of the

---

[9] Smith, *op cit.*, pp. 62-63.

[10] J. C. Bonner, *Studies in Georgia History and Government*, pp. 94-95.

[11] E. M. Coulter, *Short History of Georgia*, p. 133.

[12] There was an unprotected seacoast and danger from the Spanish in Florida. The Indians to their backs constituted a constant menace.

monarch.[13] There continued, however, to be a Commons House of Assembly whose members were elected by parishes and districts, the qualifications being that they must be twenty-one years of age, must own five hundred acres of land or property of five hundred pounds, and must not be Papist. Voters must be twenty-one years old, and must own fifty acres of land or other property of fifty pounds sterling. The members of the Commons House elected their own speaker, but the governor could negative their acts, and could even negative their elections. They elected their door-keepers and messengers but the governor appointed the clerks and adjourned, prorogued or dissolved them at his pleasure. The rules conformed to the rules of the House of Commons, and the members received no compensation.[14] Obviously this was a government of property holders, in keeping with the general tenets of the day.

Georgia benefited by the recent policy of the King in his appointment of governors—a policy deliberately adopted for the purpose of winning favor among the colonies and securing their acceptance of the appointees. Appointments were made of men of military standing or civil prestige; some had special connections in England or in the colony, some had had governmental experience. They were well received, and identified themselves with the people of the influential classes. Burdened more and more heavily with responsibilities they had little time for constitutional reform.[15] One such governor was Governor Wright of Georgia, who served from 1761 to 1776 and from 1779 to near the end of the Revolution. He was respected and loved, and there was never, even in the scene of his arrest, any violence or outrage. His term of office was notable for commercial and general prosperity.[16] The big merchants had re-

---

13 W. B. Stevens, *History of Georgia*, II, p. 94.

14 *Revolutionary Records*, III, preface pp. 3-5.

15 R. B. Morris ed., *The Era of the Revolution*, p. 267-268. They suffered financially in the Revolution.

16 Stevens, *op. cit.*, II, p. 95.

ceived bounties [17] and "the metropolis was filled with placemen." [18] The sparse population was pleased with a home government which gave them bounties, subsidies, money and presents for the Indians.[19] By warnings, pleas, and propaganda, Governor Wright kept Georgia in line long after organized resistance to British control had begun.

The Governor's strong influence for conservatism, and the loyalties of certain older men such as James Habersham and Noble Jones, prevailed until 1775; but in that year the movement led by the radicals obtained control. Its leaders were moved, not by indignation over any actual wrongs suffered by Georgia, but by fellow feeling for the other colonies. At first it looked as if the merchants as a class might hold firm, but other combinations of interest forced them into the fray. A list of people attainted by Governor Wright for rebellion includes counselors, generals, the superintendent of Indian affairs, clerks, distillers, planters, shopkeepers, yeomen, mariners, tavern-keepers, gents, sheriffs, surgeons, butchers, chaplains, secretaries, vessel masters, and bricklayers.[20]

To the other colonies it appeared that Georgia was too slow in making the change from conservative to radical. Some of the merchants endeavored to suppress the opposition to the Stamp Act. Forty merchants with their clerks and several ships' captains arrived to protect the governor. Some stamps were used. Charleston, boycotting Georgia, referred to it as " that infamous colony." [21] Gradually discord arose between the well-to-do merchants and the other inhabitants. In sympathy with general protest throughout the country against the restrictive measures of Britain, a group which called itself the Amicable So-

17 *Ibid*, II, p. 93-94. Nearly one million dollars was granted outright by Parliament.

18 Nevins, *op. cit.*, p. 48.

19 Schlesinger, *op. cit.*, p. 379.

20 The royal governments most nearly held Georgia and New York, according to E. B. Greene, *Foundations of American Nationality*, p. 206.

21 Details from Schlesinger, *op. cit.*, pp. 75-82, 147-148.

ciety met at Liberty Hall, Savannah, and decided to call a larger meeting for September 12, 1769. At this meeting the acts of Parliament complained against were declared unconstitutional and a mild form of non-importation was agreed upon. The radicals were not satisfied, however; a mass meeting was called for September 19. Here a form of association patterned after that of South Carolina was adopted—but it was not rigidly enforced. South Carolina in no uncertain terms accused Georgia of being a focus of infection for the rest of the colonies, and threatened to cut it off from the others if it did not conform.[22]

So matters stood for some time. One can imagine the situation. On the one hand there were a hundred odd merchants who because of early ties, or because of business favors, had no grudge against England. These older men who had been through the early years of hardship, and had seen Georgia bebegin and grow, now expected to live out their days in mellow satisfaction. To this group one might add the larger planters, who for much the same reasons felt the tug of loyalty to the mother country.[23] On the other hand there were scores of

[22] Hugh McCall, *History of Georgia*, II, p. 4, speaks of the dangers from Schovilites leagued with Indians, and says, "The charge of inactivity vanishes when the sword and hatchet are held over the heads of the actors to compel them to lie still."

[23] In 1773, Benjamin Andrew, one of the Dorchester-Midway settlers, owner of a rice plantation, entertained the naturalist, William Bartram. The latter's account of his visit will throw some light on the more comfortably situated residents of Georgia:

> He received and entertained me in every respect as a worthy gentleman would a stranger, that is, with hearty welcome, plain but plentiful board, free conversation and liberality of sentiment. . . The day following. . .I viewed with pleasure this gentlemen's exemplary improvements in agriculture, particularly in the growth of rice, and in his machines for shelling that valuable grain.

He also spoke of the magnolias, myrtles and sweet bay trees and of the red-belly fish they caught—in all a pleasant experience for Bartram and for Benjamin Andrew.

William Bartram, *Travels Through North and South Carolina, Georgia, Etc.*, *pp.* 11-12. (C. C. Jones, *Biographical Sketches*).

younger men, born in this country, sons of the very men above described, who were not willing to accept blindly the *status quo* in regard to constitutional rights, and who doubtless gathered many a time at Tondee's Tavern,[24] or later at the Liberty Pole, and talked among themselves, as young men will do, of the latest theories that were being propounded all over the cultured eighteenth century world, and of the news just brought by the latest packet boat. When visitors arrived from other colonies, the young folk of Georgia must have been thrilled by the discovery that all over the country our relations with England were being discussed with the same boldness as at home. Did they talk of the proper relationship between the parts of an empire, a Federal system, a written constitution, the importance of a colonial legislature as compared with the legislature in England, the indignity of being subordinated to an inferior position in the scheme of things? One can only guess. Certainly after 1770 committees of correspondence, organized by Sam Adams, were busily rallying just such young men as Joseph Habersham,[25] Noble W. Jones, and John Houstoun, all sons of Loyal fathers. So sentiment was nourished, and the rebellious spirit grew. Only an overt act was needed to crystallize action.

In July of 1774, after The Boston Tea Party, the port of Boston was closed. The *Georgia Gazette* of July 20, carried the following item:[26]

> The critical situation to which British Provinces in America are likely to be reduced, from the alarming and arbitrary impositions of the late act of the British Parliament, respecting

---

[24] Early in the struggle the long room of this tavern situated on the northeast corner of Broughton and Whitaker Streets became the headquarters of the Liberty party. The innkeeper himself is said to have stood in the doorway, admitting only those whose names appeared on his list of "Sons of Liberty".

[25] Son of the foremost business man in Savannah and a leading merchant in his own right.

[26] Stevens, *op. cit.*, p. 76.

the town of Boston, as well as the acts that at present exist tending to the raising of a perpetual revenue, without the consent of the people or their representatives, is considered as an object extremely important at this critical juncture, and particularly calculated to deprive the American subjects of their constitutional rights and liberties as parts of the British Empire.

Here was the moment waited for. Forthwith, a meeting was called at Tondee's Tavern, Savannah, on July 27th, to take up the matter, " and such other constitutional measures (pursued) as may then appear most eligible." [27] The leaders at this meeting were Noble W. Jones, Archibald Bulloch, John Houstoun, and George Walton. The attendance was good, but it was felt that there should be more men present from all the parishes, so business was postponed to August 10, and notices were sent by John Glen, chairman of the Savannah Committee of 31,[28] to the various parishes.[29] Governor Wright declared any such meeting illegal and unconstitutional. Nevertheless, the meeting was held on August 10, 1774. One finds here, for the first time in Georgia, evidence of serious discontent. Such expressions as: the colonists are "entitled to the same rights, privileges and immunities with fellow-subjects in Great Britain," "right to petition," "*ex post facto*," "no taxation without representation," have a familiar sound to one's ears. Georgians asserted that the Boston Port Bill was unconstitutional, because it deprived men of property without trial. It was a subversion of rights to abolish the Massachusetts Charter:

> We will concur with our sister colonies in every constitutional measure to obtain redress of American grievances and will by every lawful means in our power maintain those inestimable blessings for which we are indebted to God and the

---

[27] Stevens, *op. cit.*, p. 77.

[28] Later Chief Justice.

[29] *Revolutionary Records, Georgia*, I, pp. 12-13.

Constitution of our country—a Constitution founded upon reason and justice, and the indelible rights of mankind.[30]

A committee was appointed for subscription for the suffering poor of Boston,[31] 579 barrels of rice being contributed.[32] No step was taken towards sending delegates to a general convention; but, in protest against this inaction, St. John's parish, St. George's and St. David's, decided that each of them would send its own delegation. A few months later—in January of 1775, St. Andrew's parish passed a series of resolutions,[33] chose delegates to the coming Provincial Congress, and adopted articles of agreement as follows:[34]

> We do associate, under all the ties of religion, honor, and love of country, to adopt and endeavor to carry into execution, whatever may be recommended by the Continental Congress, or resolved upon by our Provincial convention that shall be appointed, for the purpose of preserving our Constitution, and opposing the execution of the several arbitrary and oppressive acts of the British Parliament until a reconciliation between Great Britain and America, on constitutional principles which we most ardently desire, can be obtained.

The Provincial Congress met at Savannah, as planned, by invitation of Christ Church Parish and John Glen, Chairman. Concurrently the General Assembly was meeting. The Council

---

30 Stevens, *op. cit.*, p. 80.

31 The Committee consisted of: William Ewen, W. Young, J. Clay, J. Houstoun, N. W. Jones, E. Telfair, J. Smith, S. Farley, A. E. Wells.

32 Stevens, *op. cit.*, p. 81.

33 *Ibid.* p. 86. (1) Approbation of people of Massachusetts and of Associations of Grand American Congress. (2) Condemnation of shutting of land offices. (3) Disapproval of mandates which prevented Colonial Assemblies from passing laws as required. (4) Reprobation of practice of making colonial officers dependent for salaries on Great Britain. (5) Disapproval of practice of slavery. (6) Choice of delegates to represent district in provincial congress and appointment of two delegates to Continental Congress in May in Philadelphia.

34 *Ibid.*, p. 87.

was loyal, while the lower house was firm in its insistence on constitutional rights. The Governor adjourned the Assembly, but the Provincial Congress proceeded, though representing only five of the parishes, to elect Noble W. Jones, (who refused to go out of deference to his Loyalist father), Archibald Bulloch and John Houstoun as delegates to the Philadelphia meeting. St. John's, angered at the unsatisfactory terms of the agreements of association, elected, in its own upright and independent fashion, Lyman Hall to represent it at Philadelphia.[35] Hall has already been mentioned as one of the outstanding citizens of the parish. He was a Yale man, a preacher turned doctor, and a successful rice planter.

In May, then, of 1775, Lyman Hall might be found in Philadelphia occupying an honored seat, though scarcely a representative of his whole colony. Six feet tall, well proportioned, affable and calm, this gentleman with the easy, polite manners probably cut quite a figure in the group he joined in Philadelphia.[36] The delegates elected at Savannah did not attend, but sent a letter stating that they did not feel themselves qualified, since they did not represent the whole colony, and that they would patiently await recommendations from the Congress.

It is not our purpose here to trace the whole story of how Georgia finally united in action against England—our object is simply to call attention to expressions of a constitutional nature. On May 10, 1775, the news of Lexington reached Savannah; action followed immediately. On June 5 the first Liberty Pole was erected. At Tondee's Tavern toasts were drunk to a speedy reconciliation, to the Earl of Chatham, to Mr. Hancock and to Dr. Franklin.[37] On June 13 [38] there was a meeting at

---

[35] *Revolutionary Records, Georgia*, I, 55-56, 59-61.

[36] Description from C. C. Jones., *Biographical Sketches of the Delegates of the Continental Congress.*

[37] J. William Harden, *A History of Savannah and South Georgia*, I, p. 168.

[38] Jones, *History* II, pp. 178-179.

the home of a Mrs. Cuyler in Savannah. Resolutions were passed, for example: "no person behaving himself peaceably and inoffensively shall be molested in his personal property or even in his private sentiments while he expresses them with decency and without any illiberal reflections upon others."

To the alarm of Governor Wright, however, the exhibition of the temper of the colony continued. There was increasing avowal of independent sentiments, and a growing tendency to place under a ban all who failed to show active sympathy with the complaints and claims of the united colonies.

On June 22, a Council of Safety was appointed.[39] On July 4, 1775, a Provincial Congress fully representative of the whole of Georgia met; Archibald Bulloch was elected President, George Walton Secretary. It was decided to conform completely to the general association of the Continental Congress, and five delegates, fully accredited this time, were sent to Philadelphia—John Houstoun, Archibald Bulloch, the Reverend Dr. J. J. Zubly, Noble W. Jones, and Lyman Hall.[40]

On July 20, Georgia at last was in accord with the other colonies, the threats to exclude it ceased, and it was *persona grata* at the Continental Congress. The rest of that year was taken up by the activities of the Council of Safety, meeting every Monday at Tondee's Tavern at 10:00 a. m. It was empowered to prevent royalists from gaining control, keep local counties and the Continental Congress informed of conditions, lay in supplies, enforce the non-importation agreements, and execute the frugality measures as adopted by the earlier Continental Congress. In November the royal courts were closed[41]

---

39 Stevens, *op. cit.*, p. 101. The members consisted of W. Ewen, President, Seth John Cuthbert, Secretary, Joseph Habersham, E. Telfair, W. LeConte, B. Cownes, J. Clay, G. Walton, J. Glenn, S. Elbert, W. Young, E. Butler, J. Houstoun, J. Smith, F. H. Harris, J. Morel.

40 *Revolutionary Records, Georgia*, I, 250.

41 A different policy had been followed by England with this last of the distant children and its welfare had been closely guarded, at first by the Proprietor, then by the Trustees, finally by King and Parliament jointly. A great respect for authority in whatsoever body it lay was developed, and

and early the next year, on January 18, 1776, Governor Wright was arrested. It would seem that Wright had for some time realized the necessity of a reform in government. In writing to Lord Dartmouth in August, 1774, he had remarked that " It may be found advisable to settle the line with respect to taxation etc. by some new mode or Constitution." [42] And a foreshadowing of things to come may be seen in a report to Lord Dartmouth in 1775, in which the Governor laments that there were

> very few men of real abilities, gentlemen or men of Property in their Tribunals. The parochial committees are a parcel of the Lowest People chiefly carpenters, shoemakers, black-

---

to Georgia authority, though formerly meaning Executive, had come to mean the Parliament. No act was passed here by the General Assembly until 1775 because of this close holding of the reins by the English Government. The judicial system used was one of town courts, the first being that of Savannah. It was supreme and there was no appeal from it. It consisted of three bailiffs and a recorder. Freeholders, only, acted as jurymen. After 1741 appeal could be had from these courts to the President and assistants for over twenty pounds and to the Trustees for over one hundred pounds. In 1743 the President and assistants were empowered as a Court of Appeals, to be overruled by the Trustees. After 1754 and until the Revolution, courts were organized under the royal governor, and a General Court meeting four times a year to handle civil business, and an Oyer and Terminer and general gaol delivery twice a year for criminal business. Subsequently these two were combined to handle all cases. If the case involved over three hundred pounds, one might appeal to the Governor, and if over five hundred pounds, to the King. Courts of Conscience took care of cases up to eight pounds, and special commissions were made up for the trial of slaves, who committed offenses, without jury. Courts of Chancery were held after each General Court, for trying equity cases, the Governor acting as Chancellor. In 1760 the first law was passed in Georgia conferring civil jurisdiction on justices of the peace, the origin of justices' courts as part of the judicial system of the State. This system became later the " Small Debts Court." From this it may be judged that attention centered in the Executive as Representative of the Crown and Parliament and not on the Judiciary. (Details prior to 1777 digested from Coulter, *op. cit., The Georgia Historical Quarterly*, VII, pp. 289-312; IX, pp. 131-158; X, pp. 222-237, pp. 251-276; J. R. McCain, *Georgia as a Proprietary colony;* W. McElreath, *A Treatise on the Constitution of Georgia.*)

42 Morris, ed., *op. cit.*, p. 262.

smiths, etc., with a Few at their Head in the General Committee of Safety, there are some better Sort of men and Some Merchants and Planters but many of the Inferior Class, and it is really Terrible my Lord that Such People should be suffered to Overturn the Civil Government and most arbitrarily determine upon, and Sport with Other Men's Lives Libertys and Propertys.[43]

It was St. John's Parish, the Midway district, which Governor Wright described as the head of the rebellion; its inhabitants were " descendants of New England people of the Puritan Independent sect who, retaining a strong tincture of Republicanism or Oliverian principles have entered into an agreement amongst themselves to adopt both the resolutions and association of the Continental Congress." [44] Four days after the arrest of the Governor the Provincial Congress under Archibald Bulloch assumed control of Georgia. The delegates named to the Continental Congress at this time were Bulloch, Houstoun, Hall, Walton, and Gwinnett. It was the last three who, in behalf of Georgia, signed their names to the Declaration of Independence.[45]

Meanwhile, in April of 1776, it appeared necessary to draw up a more definite framework of government for Georgia. As was indicated, the royal governor had been arrested and was living in more or less voluntary imprisonment, (from which he later fled to a vessel in the harbor, to return to Savannah in 1799 for the duration of the war, thus forcing the removal of the patriot center into the interior).[46] So a Constitution for

[43] *Ibid.*, p. 265.

[44] C. C. Jones., *The Dead Towns of Georgia*, p. 176.

[45] Bulloch was only occasionally in attendance at the Continental Congress, being kept busy as governor in Georgia. John Houstoun would have signed the Declaration but he had returned to Georgia to counteract the work of the Reverend Zubly who was trying to defeat the Revolutionary movement.

[46] The capital of the State was in Savannah from 1777-1778. From 1778 to 1784 it was located at Augusta except for two terms spent at Head's Fort (now Washington) and Ebenezer for safety's sake during the war. In

## PRE-REVOLUTIONARY GEORGIA

Georgia was drawn up by the Provincial Congress, to serve as a frame until a more stable form could be arranged. This was Georgia's first Constitution, then premature since it still was technically a colony, but bearing some interesting features to be worked out in more detail after its Statehood was declared. For instance, in the Preamble, it was declared that there are certain liberties given by God and the Constitution, that these were in a precarious condition since the suspension of the old form of government, and that this temporary arrangement would meet the immediate and urgent need for a basic law. The Provincial Congress, meantime, was to represent the people, " with whom all power originates."

The framework consisted of a President (Commander-in-Chief) with executive powers, appointed by ballot in the Provincial Congress for six months, and a Council of Safety of thirteen besides the five delegates to the General Congress, to serve as a Privy Council. All legislative power was secured to the Provincial Congress and no person holding any civil or military commission was to sit in it. A Chief Justice, two assistant Judges, Attorney General, Provost-Marshal, and Clerk of the Court of Sessions were to be appointed by ballot (with salary scales arranged).[47] While the President and Council could appoint parish officials, all laws, common or statute, and acts of the Assembly formerly acknowledged, and all resolves of the Continental and Provincial Congresses were to be in force.[48] As one can see, there are here the beginnings of ideas which are later worked out, such as separation of powers, em-

---

1784 the official government was again in Savannah. Back in Augusta in 1785 and 1786, the legislators passed an act in 1786 authorizing the selection of a site for the permanent capital. In 1796 the selection of Louisville was made. Later, removals were to Milledgeville, and to Atlanta in 1868. The final selection was authorized by a vote taken upon an ordinance attached to the work of the Constitutional Convention of 1877.

[47] President 300 pounds, Chief Justice 100 pounds, Attorney General 25 pounds, Provost-Marshall 60 pounds, Clerk of Court 50 pounds.

[48] Bulloch was again elected President. John Glen was Chief Justice, William Stephens Attorney General, and James Jackson Clerk of Court.

phasis upon the legislature, a conservatism in judiciary techniques.

The one major difference between this and a peacetime situation was that it was necessary to lean heavily on the executive and his council. These men were going to have to assume temporarily some of the functions of a national government, such as the issuance of paper money, naval protection, and alien restrictions. On February 22, 1777, the President was even ordered " to take upon himself the whole executive powers of government, calling to his assistance not less than five persons of his own choosing to consult and advise with him on every urgent occasion, when a sufficient number of councillors cannot be convened to make a board." [49]

While Georgia was thus organizing for pursuit of the course it had at last decided upon, the members of the Continental Congress were proceeding to the business in hand—the working out of a declaration to end the situation of a war undeclared since April of 1775. On July 4, the Declaration of Independence was signed at Philadelphia and the news borne homeward. On August 8, the Declaration was delivered into the hands of President Bulloch in Savannah, where it was announed on August 10 in the *Universal Intelligencer* (printed by Timothy Green.) [50]

Savannah (in Georgia)
August 10th, 1776

A Declaration being received from the Honorable John Hancock, Esq., by which it appeared that The Continental Congress, in the name, and by the authority of their constituents, had declared that the United Colonies of North America are, and of right ought to be Free and Independent States, and absolved from all allegiance to the British crown, his Excellency the President and the Honorable Council met in the Council Chamber and read the Declaration.

[49] Stevens, *op. cit.*, p. 155.
[50] George White, *Historical Collections*, pp. 200-201.

They then proceeded to the square before the Assembly House, and read it to a great concourse of people, when the grenadier and light infantry companies fired a general volley. After this they proceeded in the following processions to the Liberty Pole: The grenadiers in front—the provost marshall on horseback, with his sword drawn—the Secretary, with the Declaration—His Excellency, the President—the Honorable, the Council and gentlemen attending—then the light infantry, and the rest of the militia of the town and district of Savannah. At the Liberty Pole they were met by ten Georgia battalions, who, after reading of the Declaration, discharged their field-pieces, and fired in platoons, upon this they proceeded to the battery, at the Trustee's gardens, where the Declaration was read for the last time, and the cannons of the battery discharged. His Excellency and Council, Col. Lachlin McIntosh and other gentlemen with the militia, dined under the cedar trees, and cheerfully drank to the United, True and Independent States of America. In the evening the town was illuminated, and there was exhibited a very solemn funeral procession, attended by the grenadier and light infantry companies, and other militia, with their drums muffled, and fifes and a greater number of people than ever appeared on any occasion before in this Province, when George the Third was interred before the Court House in the following manner:—

For as much as George the Third, of Great Britain, hath most flagrantly violated his Coronation oath, and trampled upon the Constitution of our country, and the sacred rights of mankind: We therefore commit his political existence to the ground—corruption to corruption—tyranny to the grave —and oppression to eternal infamy; in wise and certain hopes that he will never obtain a resurrection to rule again over these United States of America. But, my friends and fellow-citizens, let us not be sorry, or men without hope, for tyrants that thus depart, rather let us remember America is free and independent; that she is, and will be with the blessing of the Almighty Great among the nations of the earth. Let this encourage us in well doing, to fight for our rights and our privileges, for our wives and children, for all that is near and dear and so may God give us his blessing and let all the people say Amen.

Georgia, as one of the thirteen free states, enjoyed the celebration of its freedom that night. The next morning brought more sober thoughts,—there was a war to be fought and won, and a permanent government to be set up. It is probable, however, that no fear was felt on either score, for the men who had guided affairs for the last few years stood by, ready to lend their statesmanship and the wisdom born of experience.

## CHAPTER II
## THE FRAMING OF THE FIRST STATE CONSTITUTION

WITH the acceptance of the Declaration of Independence, Georgia became officially a republic. By a resolution passed on May 15, 1776, a copy of which was sent to each of the thirteen republics, the Continental Congress had recommended that each of these young republics call a meeting at which fairly chosen representatives should draft a new Constitution if the present frame of government were not suitable to the exigencies of the time. In Georgia the idea of a separate constitutional convention to frame the fundamental law seems not to have developed just yet. An act, reenacted on December 8, 1775, indicated that the number of delegates was fixed at 96, the number of districts at 18, the franchise belonging to every man who paid a tax. This act provided that election to the Provincial Congress should be by ballot, and that free holders should be qualified to serve as delegates.

The Assembly not being in session, President Bulloch sent out a call for a new election, and the men elected in response to his call came together in Savannah at a meeting which was not specifically a constitutional convention, but rather a session of the General Assembly. The proclamation set the election of delegates between the first and tenth days of September, 1776, and the meeting for the first Tuesday in October, "when business of the highest consequence to the government and welfare of the State will be opened for their consideration." [1] A circular letter sent out to the parishes emphasized the necessity for the selection of upright men, friends to freedom, and of some political judgment.[2]

Elections were duly held and the delegates assembled, as called, in October. Since these men were also the Assembly, with

[1] *Revolutionary Records, Georgia*, II, 281.
[2] *Ibid.*

many war duties, they did not proceed rapidly with their main task; but on February 5, 1777, that task was completed.[3] The Constitution was signed, adopted, and promulgated by the so-called convention without the ratification of the voters of the State. It was for twelve years the organic law of the State, "a strange medley of a new Democracy and respect for old forms."[4]

When Allen D. Candler collected the *Revolutionary Records of Georgia* in 1908, he announced that, to his distress, no journal of the proceedings of the meeting of 1776-1777 was still in existence, or any list of the members; but, he said, the Constitution itself was the record of the work which they did "without model or precedent." Later historians are more fortunate. A fragment of the minutes has been found, attached to a copy of the Constitution printed at Savannah by William Lancaster in 1777.[5] The fragment contains some of the minutes of the meeting of the committee selected to prepare the Constitution, a committee consisting of Button Gwinnett, William Belcher, Joseph Wood, Reverend Josiah Lewis, John Adam Treutlen, Henry Jones, and George Wells. The biographer of Button Gwinnett[6] adds several other names of delegates to this list, including Joseph Clay and John Appling. To these may be added Edward Langworthy, who signed the minutes as Secretary, and possibly William Few (whose name was given in White's *Historical Collections*).

The entire make-up of this first body of Constitution-framers is not known, but enough is known to reconstruct a large

---

[3] Several other states had completed their constitutions prior to the assembling of the Georgia group. New York and Georgia were delayed, by various external and internal dangers, in following the others, New Hampshire, South Carolina, Virginia, New Jersey, Delaware, Pennsylvania, North Carolina. Nevins, *op. cit.*, p. 128.

[4] *Georgia Bar Association Reports* 1921, p. 213.

[5] Pierpont Morgan Library.

[6] Charles Francis Jenkins, *Button Gwinnett—Signer of the Declaration of Independence*.

FRAMING OF FIRST STATE CONSTITUTION    31

part of the picture. First of all, there was Button Gwinnett, back from the Continental Congress, fresh from the thrilling experience of attending the debates which preceeded the adoption of the Declaration. Born in England, Gwinnett had settled in Georgia and by 1765 was doing such a prosperous business as a merchant that he purchased St. Catherine's Island near the port of Sunbury. A leader, both at home and throughout the colonies, it is natural that Gwinnett should have taken a prominent part in the drafting of the Constitution. One notes that Lyman Hall, George Walton, and Bullock[7] were absent, but it is reasonably certain that William Few was there.[8]

Among those present were Joseph Wood, a planter of the Sunbury settlement, and Joseph Clay, a Princeton graduate and Baptist clergyman who later was to serve in the revising Convention of 1795 and in the Convention of 1798, and who was to be legislated out of office in the repeal of the " mid-

[7] Since February 2, Walton had served as a delegate in the Continental Congress. He was to remain a delegate (with brief intervals for army service), until 1781. This dignified, reserved, comely statesman gave of himself in many capacities. After the war Walton again appeared briefly as governor, then as member of the Constitutional Convention of 1788, as governor again, as judge of the Superior Court and as senator. (Description from C. C. Jones, *Biographical Sketches*).

Archibald Bullock was, one assumes, busy exercising the dictatorial powers granted for the conduct of the war. Perhaps he would not have been acceptable on the floor of this Assembly since, according to the provisions of the temporary Constitution under which they were living, no officer, civil or military, was supposed to sit in the house.

Lyman Hall's plantation and home were seized and destroyed when the British took Savannah and he went north again, remaining until the peace. Then he returned to Georgia to practice medicine and to become governor. Though Hall was not a member of the Committee and asserted that he had no hand in the Constitution, he expressed himself as pleased with it in a letter to Roger Sherman of July 16, 1777. (Pierpont Morgan Library). He did not deny its imperfections, but thought it contained provisions for equal justice and liberty.

[8] William Few was a lawyer, born in England of Quaker stock. He had moved to Georgia via Pennsylvania, Maryland and North Carolina. His experiences on this committee served him in good stead when he later attended the Federal Constitutional Convention. He was to move, some years later, to New York, there to live as a valued public servant.

night judges" act. John Adam Treutlen was there, a Salzburger of the Ebenezer settlement who was destined to be elected first governor under the new document. When the Tories later seized Savannah, he escaped to South Carolina, where, according to report, he was drawn and quartered by the Tories. Finally there was Edward Langworthy, born near Savannah and raised in the Bethesda orphanage, a teacher favoring the Loyalist side, but reversing himself to serve in various capacities in the State; as a member of the Continental Congress, he was one of the three Georgia signers of the Articles of Confederation.[9]

On January 24, 1777, so one learns from the fragment attached to the Constitution of 1777, a committee of seven was chosen by ballot to reconsider and revise the form of a Constitution heretofore proposed and reported (by which one judges there had been some debate, proposal, and counter-proposal). On January 29, Gwinnett brought in the report, which was read once. On January 30 it was read again and on January 31 for the third time. On February 1, it was considered paragraph by paragraph, and on February 3, the House took the whole draft under consideration, and debated it. After a final reading on February 4, it was voted unanimously. Five hundred copies were ordered to be printed, with the Act of Distribution and the *Habeas Corpus* Act of Charles II's time annexed. The Committee which had worked on the Constitution was ordered to supervise the printing.

Of one other occurrence at the meetings there is record.[10] In the winter of 1776 the legislature of South Carolina passed a resolution proposing union with Georgia. A committee with William Henry Drayton as chairman, was sent to Georgia to request a hearing at the Convention on the subject of this proposal. The request was granted early in January, but after a courteous hearing, the proposal was turned down. Drayton

---

9 The other two were John Walton and Edward Telfair.

10 *Revolutionary Records*, I, 309.

attributed the failure to the leadership of Gwinnett, and proceeded to attack him and other members of the convention.[11] Nevertheless, Georgia stuck to its decision to stand alone, and issued its Constitution accordingly.

In analyzing this first Georgia Constitution, one is tempted, at first, to assume that it was too simple,[12] and that it merely retained, with some changes, the government by which Georgia had been living. Yet it had virtues which later Constitution-makers might well have imitated—simplicity of style, brevity, and adherence to the barest fundamentals; it was really a Constitution, not a code of laws. For the twelve years during which it functioned, it worked well.

In analyzing the early Constitutions, some authorities have indicated that North Carolina and Georgia were the most democratic states of the South.[13] Georgia gave almost complete control to the legislature of one house. Other estimates list Georgia with North Carolina, Delaware, and Pennsylvania as most nearly attaining the democratic ideal.[14] Perhaps all the states drew from the same eighteenth century doctrines of natural right, separation of powers, consent of the governed, English charters and the Bill of Rights. Perhaps, too, the fact that so many of Georgia's Revolutionary leaders were members of the bar, many of whom had been educated in the North, may account for the provisions similar to those in other states.[15]

---

11 After Gwinnett's death, Drayton circulated a paper reflecting on him and his associates. Governor Treutlen therefore, on July 15, 1777 issued a proclamation of a reward of 100 pounds for the arrest of Drayton.

12 "If the framework had been more creditable, we would be more willing to credit the sagacious Archibald Bulloch with it." So says A. Nevins, *op. cit.*, p. 138.

13 Nevins, *op. cit.*, p. 195.

14 Curtis Nettels, *Roots of American Civilization*, p. 665.

15 Members of the bar among Revolutionary leaders: J. Houstoun, J. Glen, W. Ewen, W. Gibbon, J. Rutledge, E. Telfair, J. A. Treutlen, B. Taliaferro, W. Few, L. Hall, A. Baldwin.

# CHAPTER III
# LEARNING BY TRIAL AND ERROR

### I. First State Constitution

THE first Constitution made its public appearance in Savannah on February 5, 1777, " in the first year of independence of the United States of America." [1] Consisting of an introduction which might be called a Preamble, and sixty-three articles arranged in no particular sequence, it shows evidence of haste. For the purpose of this discussion, the articles have been arranged by topic: Preamble, Legislature, Executive, Judiciary and Miscellaneous.

The Preamble approaches a statement of fundamental principles of government. This is no bill of rights, nor will one be found anywhere in this document, since the rights and privileges usually associated with this phrase are scattered throughout its pages. There was no occasion for enumerating them at the start. The men at the convention were not representatives of masses of unenfranchised people, proclaiming some radical seizure of hitherto unheard-of power. They were speaking primarily for the enfranchised freeholders of a community whose privileges had, they felt, been invaded. The representatives averaged, perhaps, one man for every two hundrd and fifty white people, most of whom probably owned some acres or had some business interests. For those who had nothing, they would speak, however, and they did speak.

Starting out by blaming, not King George, as the Declaration of Independence had done, but " the Legislature of Great Britain " for having lately asserted the right to raise taxes and to bind them by all sorts of laws " repugnant to the common rights of mankind " the Preamble recalled that the Americans had had to assert themselves in regard to the rights and priv-

[1] H. Marbury and W. H. Crawford, *Digest of the Laws of the State of Georgia.*

ileges to which they were entitled by the laws of nature and reason. Consequently, in accordance with the recommendations of Congress, the delegates were establishing a government which would " best conduce to the happiness and safety of their constituents in particular and America in general." Since independence had been declared and all political connection with the Crown of Great Britain had been dissolved, they therefore, as " the representatives of the people, from whence all power originates and for whose benefit all government is intended ", in accordance with their power delegated by the people, declared the Constitution of sixty-three articles adopted for the government of the State.

Separation of the three departments of government was provided "so that neither exercised the powers properly belonging to the other." This was easier said than done and was not followed throughout the rest of the document, or in practice thereafter.[2] While the framework of the government was divided into three parts, there was no question which was closest to the hearts of framers. The governor was too much associated in their minds with royal control. The judiciary, held down by revision by the Privy Council, governor's whim or transfer of jurisdiction to England, had not developed its position as it was later to do. It was to the legislature that these men entrusted the real government of the new State. Even here, provisions for election and tenure kept control constantly in the hands of the people. Legislative authority was vested in a single house. The " representatives of the people " were to be elected yearly on the first Tuesday in December and were to

[2] Quite early arose the questions of violation of this principle. (a) Cooper v. Telfair (4 Dallas U. S. 14) is the first case of a justice discussing the right to hold a state law unconstitutional. (b) When Savannah was evacuated in 1783, General Wayne tried to procure from Governor Martin an assurance that the persons and property of any persons who saw fit to remain in town should be protected, but the governor declined to enter into this "alleging that the Executive and Judiciary were separate and distinct, and that over the latter he had no control." White, *op. cit.*, p. 214.

meet at Savannah on the first Tuesday in January.[3] The unalterable rule was that each year's House should expire on the day before the election for the next one. There was no opportunity for long tenure such as had been common in colonial times.

On the first day of the meeting in January, the legislature was to elect a governor. It was also to select, out of its own number, an Executive Council, choosing by ballot two from each county except that a county not entitled to send ten delegates had no representation. The members not elected to the Council were to constitute the House.

## II. The Legislature

Let us examine further the legislative department. What were its qualifications, rights and powers? How was it to be assembled? The principle of allotment used was based upon size of electorate rather than population. The old parishes were renamed counties and a fixed number of representatives was assigned to each of them. Each county was to keep its own records.[4] In the apportionment, Liberty County was allowed fourteen representatives, Glynn and Camden one each, the other counties ten each. The City of Savannah was given four,

---

[3] "Or elsewhere" must have been added in order to make sure of the continuance of a stable government even if, in a war emergency, its seat should have to be removed.

[4] It is interesting to note the names of the counties. As "the Convention was not unmindful of the debt of gratitude to distinguished statesmen and friends in England, who had espoused the cause of justice, humanity, and liberty," several counties were given names in evidence of this debt (Jones, *History of Georgia*, II, p. 255). Christ Church and part of St. Philip's became Chatham County (for William Pitt) with Savannah as the largest town; upper St. Philip's and all of St. Matthew's became Effingham (for the opponent of Lord North), St. George's became Burke, St. Paul's Richmond (for Charles Lennox), with Augusta its main city; St. Thomas' and St. Mary's became Camden (for Charles Pratt, Chief Justice and Chancellor); St. David's and St. Patrick's became Glynn (for the defender of John Wilkes). The lands north of the Ogeechee were formed into Wilkes; St. John's, St. Andrew's and St. James' became Liberty, with four major centers, Midway, Sunbury, Darien, Frederica.

the town of Sunbury two—"to represent their trade." Further provision was made for Glynn, for Camden and for future counties: though they were to have, at the start, one member for ten electors, they might in future have two for thirty, three for forty, four for fifty and ten for a hundred or more. And since these two counties were " in a state of alarm," they might choose one member from any other county to represent them until they had enough residents of their own to qualify for more. This was a war measure, and would not otherwise have been acceptable under the principles for which they were fighting.[5]

The representatives chosen from these counties were to have been twelve months resident in the State and three months in the county (except in the case of Glynn and Camden as above set forth). They must be Protestant (this restriction was removed after the Revolution),[6] twenty-one years old, and possessed of two hundred and fifty acres of land, or of other property worth not less than two hundred and fifty pounds. They were not to hold any other office of profit in the State, or military commission, except officers of the militia. No clergyman was to sit in the House—a prohibition which may possibly have been aimed at the Reverend Mr. Zubly, who had left the Continental Congress to change sides and become Loyalist.[7]

[5] In *Colonial Records* (*Journal* Commons House of Assembly) XV, 123-124, is found an instance in 1769 where, when four new parishes had not been given representation in the House, the House refused to act on taxation, since this would have been inconsistent with the principles for which the colonies were then contending.

[6] " It was apparently violated at once for a member from Chatham County in 1777 was said to be Catholic." Reba C. Strickland, *Religion and the State in Georgia in the Eighteenth Century*, p. 164.

[7] Though other states had similar prohibitions, South Carolina seems to have been the only one to give a reason, explaining that ministers being dedicated to holy service, they ought not to be diverted from their business. Jenkins, *op. cit.*, p. 115. The provision disappears with the Constitution of 1798.

The House had power to make all such laws and regulations as were not repugnant to the true meaning and intent of the Constitution, and were conducive to the order and well being of the State, and to repeal all laws and ordinances injurious to the people. It might choose its speaker and other officers, make its own rules, direct writs of elections for vacancies, and adjourn itself. It was to appoint justices of the peace and registers of probate,[8] and it might call any officer of the State to account. It might authorize pleading in the courts of the State and might suspend anyone for malpractice. Finally, it might issue a call for a convention for any constitutional change, provided, however, the petitions from the counties had been received.

Any laws and ordinances it might make were to be read three times, on three different days ("except in cases of great necessity and danger"), and, after the second reading, were to be sent to the Executive Council "for their perusal and advice."

Obviously, the composition of the House was considered of primary importance, and careful provisions were made for the election of members. All male whites who were twenty-one years old, possessed of ten pounds, and liable for taxes in the State, and all mechanics of any trade who had been residents for six months, not only might vote, but must vote, subject to a maximum penalty of five pounds for absence without a reasonable excuse. Voting had to be by ballot, and no proxy was allowed.[9] In order that all elections might be "free and open", voters were to be free from process-servers or other hindrance while going to, attending, and returning from elec-

---

[8] Estates were not to be entailed. If a man died intestate, there must be an equal division among the children, the widow getting a child's share or her dower. Estates of intestates not survived by wife or child were to be treated according to the act of Distribution of Charles II unless the legislature should alter this in future.

[9] It is thought this clause was inserted because of an unfortunate duel that had taken place, over a proxy vote, the Habersham-Hughes affair, in which Hughes had been killed. Jenkins, *op. cit.*, p. 114.

tions, and no military officer or soldier might attend an election in his military character. There was to be no plural voting. Each person must vote in his own county, except that citizens of Glynn and Camden might, during the troublous wartime, vote elsewhere. Not only were titles abolished, but the holder of a title must formally relinquish it before he could vote or hold office.[10] Voters were to take an oath of allegiance to the State and to its Constitution. A Quaker could simply "affirm." Thus a Quaker could vote, but he could not hold office in the legislative or executive branch because no provision was there made for any affirmation.

Due provision was made for registration of voters and for handling returns. The ballots were to be taken by two or more justices of the peace in each county, who were to provide a convenient box. Ballots were to be compared, in public, with the list of voters and the result immediately declared, one certificate being given to the person elected and another forwarded to the House of Representatives.

When any five duly elected representatives should assemble they might administer the oath to each other and then to all the other members of the House. They were to swear allegiance to the State and to the Constitution, swear they had not obtained their election by fraud or bribe, and promise to fulfill their duties truly. It was left for the House to provide, by subsequent legislation, for the voiding of titles, and to decide upon methods of collecting, and ways of appropriating, the fines paid in for failure to exercise the franchise.

### III. THE EXECUTIVE

On the first day of its session, the House was to have the privilege of electing the governor. The position in Georgia was one of honor and respect, possibly a carry-over from the colonial period, but the man himself would have been a puppet ex-

---

[10] Probably aimed at Sir Patrick Houstoun and other titled men. Jenkins, *op. cit.*, p. 115.

cept for the war emergency. He was to be styled "honorable."[11] Wherever he resided (and his residence was to be chosen by the House) he was always to be attended by a sufficient number of members of the Executive Council—at least one from each county represented on the Council. He was to execute the laws, but in no case pardon criminals or remit fines. He might reprieve a criminal or suspend a fine only until the next meeting of the Assembly, which he had power to summon with the advice of the Council. Neither in Georgia nor elsewhere could the governor adjourn the Assembly. "The memory of the royal governors with their great influence and broad powers was still vivid and alarming." [12]

With the advice of the Council, the governor might fill intermediate vacancies until the next general election and he was to give all commissions, civil or military, under the great seal of the State. To preside over the Executive Council was his privilege except on days when they were considering laws presented " for their perusal and advice " by the House. This eliminated any direct control over legislation. No veto power was given him.

Elections for governor were annual. After residence of three years in the State, a candidate was eligible for this office only one year out of three.[13] He must not hold any military commission in any other State. Included in the oath he must take were promises to support the State, the Constitution, and the rights of the people, to execute the laws and justice "in mercy," and to "peaceably and quietly resign" at the end of his term. He must make this oath to the speaker of the Assembly; the speaker also must administer it to the president of the Council,

11 This was a part of the traditions of the past. For other practices, see the chapter entitled, " Rules of Precedency for Settlement of Precedency of Men and Women in America " in the book entitled *Conditions of British Colonies in America* published in England in 1779 by Anthony Stokes, Chief Justice, after his escape from Savannah.

12 Jenkins, *op. cit.*, pp. 111-112.

13 The term was changed to two years in 1789. Only in 1824 was the governor chosen by the qualified electorate.

who, in the governor's absence, was to serve in his place. It was provided that, whenever business of a secret nature was being debated by governor and Council, the governor should require an oath from the council members, the secretary, and any other officers necessary to carry out the business, that they would not divulge it until the Council or Assembly gave leave.

The governor " for the time being," was to be captain-general and commander-in-chief of all militia, and of any other military and naval forces belonging to the State.

The Executive Council, the other half of the plural executive system, were to meet on the day after their election and to choose a president from among their number. They were to appoint any other officers and make their own rules. Votes taken in Council should be by counties, not individuals, but a member had the right to enter a protest against measures to which he had not assented, provided he did so in three days.

While the House was sitting, the whole Council except for any members who were sick or absent because of some other urgent necessity, must be available. A majority should constitute a board to examine the laws referred to the Council by the House, and must return the laws in five days with remarks.[14] When a committee from the Council went before the House to propose amendments, they were to deliver their reasons for such proposals " sitting and covered; the whole house at that time, except the speaker, uncovered." Any transactions between legislature and governor should be carried on by a committee; between governor and House by the secretary of Council; between Council and House by a committee of Council.[15]

[14] It should be remembered that it was at these sessions that the governor was not to be present.

[15] The governors who served under this first Constitution were:

| | | |
|---|---|---|
| J. A. Treutlen . 1777 | J. Martin ..... 1782 | G. Mathews .... 1787 |
| J. Houstoun ... 1778 | L. Hall ....... 1783 | G. Handley .... 1788 |
| T. Glasscock ... 1779 | J. Houstoun ... 1784 | G. Walton ..... 1789 |
| R. Howley ..... 1780 | G. Elbert ...... 1785 | |
| N. Brownson .. 1781 | E. Telfair ...... 1786 | |

## IV. The Judiciary

Under this first State Constitution, the judiciary was the weakest branch. However, though it was dependent on the legislature and many of the provisions in regard to it were violations of the idea of separation of powers, it was probably adequate in the years during which it functioned. Most of the provisions have since been dropped but that of the Superior Court has been retained to the present day.

In each county there was to be a Superior Court which was to meet twice a year. If there were not enough inhabitants to form a court, a case must be tried in the next adjacent county where there was a court. These meetings were arranged in definite sequence beginning the first Tuesday in March and running through April, like courts to be scheduled in October and November. All causes of whatsoever nature, except those reserved for other specific courts, were to be tried by what was called a Supreme Court, consisting of a Chief Justice [16] and three or more of the justices residing in the county in which the case arose. If the Chief Justice were absent, the senior judge was to act, with the clerk, the attorney for the State, the sheriff, the coroner, the constable and the jurors. If any of the aforementioned were absent, the justices were to appoint others.[17]

Cases were to be tried in the county where the dispute arose if both parties lived in the same county, otherwise in the county of the defendant, except that land cases must be tried where

---

[16] The following men served in this capacity during the period of the first Constitution:

| | | | |
|---|---|---|---|
| J. Glen | 1776-1780 | J. Houstoun | 1786 |
| W. Stephens | 1780 | W. Stith | 1786-1787 |
| J. Wereat | 1781 | N. Pendleton | 1787-1788 |
| A. Burke | 1782 | H. Osborn | 1788-1789 |
| R. Howley | 1782 | N. Pendleton | 1789 |
| G. Walton | 1783-1786 | | |

[17] The Constitution does not say how the judges should be appointed, but presumably this was done by the Assembly.

## LEARNING BY TRIAL AND ERROR

the land lay. All matters, civil and criminal, were to come before the Supreme Court, where the jury was to judge of the law as of the facts, and must not bring in a special verdict. If the jury were in doubt about a point of law, it might refer the question to the judges, each judge in turn would then give his opinion. The jury was sworn to bring in a verdict according to the law and its opinion of the evidence and in conformity with the Constitution. Grand juries were to consist of not less than eighteen men, and twelve might draw up a bill. No cost was to exceed three pounds and no case was to be held over for more than two terms.

If either party in a suit felt dissatisfied with the outcome, he might, within three days, enter an appeal and demand a new trial by a special jury from whose decision there would be no further appeal. The special jury was sworn to bring in a verdict according to the law and its opinion, which should not be repugnant to justice, equity, conscience, and the Constitution " of which they shall judge." [18] The method of selection of the special jury merits description. Each side was to choose six names, six more names were to be taken out of a box provided for drawing of jurors. All eighteen persons so chosen were to be summoned, and their names put in a box, the twelve whose names were first drawn to be the special jury.

For the trial of cases of capture by sea or land and all maritime cases there was to be a special court called by the Chief Justice or the senior justice of the county upon application of either party, and the case had to be decided within ten days. Proceeding and appeal were to be as in other types of cases, except that after a second trial the final appeal was to the Continental Congress. The time between first and second trials was to be no more than fourteen days.[19]

---

[18] This seems to be the earliest official recognition of a review of the grounds of cases in the light of their constitutionality. It would not seem to be a foreshadowing of judicial review in the sense of a judiciary reviewing acts of a legislature.

[19] Probably the oldest complete record of a judicial proceeding in Georgia is that of John White *v.* Peter Knight, tried by Judge Glen (Chief Justice)

Courts of Conscience [20] were continued, with jurisdiction in cases involving not more than ten pounds. Georgia seems to have been the first to include the provision of limitation of jurisdiction according to the money value of the claim.

There are references to another type of small claims court recognized at the time—the Court-merchant. Ordinarily, in all cases involving not more than five pounds, a " stay of execution " could be obtained, until the first Monday in the following March, provided security were given. Anyone might profit by this except in cases subject to the jurisdiction of the "Court-merchant." The Court-merchant dated from the time when merchants, dealers and others might bring suit against transients, shipmasters, super-cargoes, and others—and have their cases tried at seven days notice,[21] such cases being tried by the Chief Justice or by one of the county justices.

No pleading (except by a man in his own defense) was to be done but by those authorized by the House. [22]

---

as Judge of the Court of Admiralty. It was the case of the capture of the sloop " Polly " Appealed to the Continental Congress, it was referred to a committee consisting of James Wilson, John Adams and T. Burke. *Georgia Bar Association Reports,* 1913, pp. 72-73.

20 Bouvier defines Courts of Conscience (or Courts of Request) as Courts of Equity for poor suitors or for the king's servants privileged to sue there. Originally a standing committee of the Council, its members were the same as those of the Star Chamber. It later became a separate court and its regular judges were called Masters of Request.

21 *Georgia Bar Association Reports,* 1921, p. 210.

22 In the earliest days of the colony, the courts had been lawyerless. Each man plead his own case. There were one or two in the colony who knew something of law, referred to as "a pretended lawyer" or "a smatterer in law." During the time of the Trustees there was no practitioner and the courts were not authorized to admit persons to the bar. In fact the absence of lawyers was given as one of the inducements for emigrating to the new colony. But a majority of the male inhabitants signed a petition, a "narration under oath," claiming that for want of legal aid "the miserable inhabitants were exposed to a more arbitrary government than was ever exercised in Turkey or Muscovy " (McCall, Hugh, *op. cit.,* I, 54). Only in 1754 did Georgia courts admit attorneys to practice. The first lawyer was William Clifton (attorney-general), student of Gray's Inn, who said there

# LEARNING BY TRIAL AND ERROR 45

One further provision was made that there should be a court house and a jail in each county, (the county seat to be chosen by the convention or by later legislation).[23]

## V. MISCELLANEOUS

Let us turn to the remaining items in the first Constitution. First, schools were to be established in each county, at state expense. Thus the State assumed responsibility for education, the method to be decided upon by future legislation. Second, a great seal of State was to be made and an elaborate scheme was worked out for both sides.[24] Button Gwinnett is thought to have made the plans. On one side was to be a scroll engraved with "The Constitution of the State of Georgia" and the motto "*Pro bono publico.*" On the other side was to be depicted an elegant house and buildings, fields of corn and meadows of sheep and cattle; a river with a ship under full sail and the motto, "*Deus Nobis Haec Otia Fecit.*"

---

was "one other of the Profession" but it is not known who he was. There was, for admission to practice, a fee of two pounds. What the requirements were is not known, but it is thought the English courts authorized those who had read law five years. Three colonial governors were lawyers and there came to be a number who had studied in England. (*Georgia Bar Association Reports,* 1913, p. 65).

Why the power of admission of lawyers was taken away from the courts in 1777 and given to the House is not known. One might say a word here, however, as to the system developed for admission to the bar. A young aspiring lawyer was "articled as a clerk" for some five years, and though one does not know the fee he paid in Georgia to read in some office, in other states, it was one hundred dollars. After twelve months residence in the State, he could take his examination, which was an oral examination in open court (*Georgia Bar Association Reports,* 1913, pp. 81-83). This practice continued for a hundred years. As a result of charges of partiality and corruption, it was finally given up and thereafter candidates were required to pass a written examination in which anonymity was insisted upon.

23 The first home rule law in Georgia was brought about by a decision before George Walton and William Few as to whether the courthouse of Richmond County should be at Kiokee, Brownsville or Augusta. *Georgia Bar Association Reports,* 1913, p. 74.

24 Jenkins, *op. cit.,* p. 10.

Finally, (and one might have started with this but for the fact that the framers did not do so themselves, but rather ended with it), certain rights were guaranteed. Religion was to be free " provided it be not repugnant to the peace and safety of the State," and no one should be required to support any teacher except of his own profession.[25] Any one should be entitled to plead his own cause in the courts, he should not be afflicted with excessive bail or fines, he should have the rights of *habeas corpus,* freedom of the press, and trial by jury.

There was no question, seemingly, of a submission of this document to a vote of the people. It seems reasonable to assume that each delegate there knew personally every man, woman and child, in the community he represented, that he had probably discussed each question of government in the city street, the crossroads store, at the farm fence, on court days, on Sundays, while hunting, fishing, drinking, eating. He probably did not once doubt that what he said and did at the meeting was the will of his constituency. This conclusion that the ultimate sovereignty was in the people is borne out in the final sentence in the document where provision was made for alteration. No alteration was to be made except by petition from a majority of counties, wherein a majority of the voters of each county had signed the petition. Only then was a convention to be ordered by the Assembly, which would vote on the specific alterations which had been proposed. Georgia and Massachusetts alone of the early States made adequate provision for alteration, and though Georgia never made use thereafter of the system devised, it is worth noting that here was the first suggestion in any American state that legislation should spring from the people.[26]

[25] This, of course, paved the way for taxation for support of one's religion, and such a law was passed in 1785; but it was never enforced.

[26] *Georgia Bar Association Reports,* 1921, p. 212.

## VI. Estimate

It is difficult to estimate the value of this first Constitution. It was formed under stress and it functioned during an exceedingly difficult time, while the officers of the State were being chased from pillar to post and the seat of government had to be repeatedly changed. It served its day; but it did not long remain unaltered. Certain it is that the unicameral legislature was shortly dropped, as well as the plural executive. The weak judiciary was later strengthened, and real democracy, only hinted at here, was gradually to be worked out. The assumption by the State of powers which belong to a Federal Government had to be given up; for example, the handling of captures, and control of an army and a navy.[27]

A characteristic of the revolutionary constitutions was that they were small in size, a mere framework. Their political philosophy was not original, but influenced largely by seventeenth century developments in England, and eighteenth century writers. The Declaration of Independence furnished some of the common clauses for justification, the committees of correspondence probably contributed others. Though Georgia had no specific bill of rights, eight states did have. Maryland, Virginia, North Carolina and Georgia expressed a separation of powers, though Georgia failed to put this into practice. The greatest divergence between the early state constitutions was in the legislature; only Pennsylvania, Vermont and Georgia used the unicameral system. Common to all was the overweaning power given to the assembly. In Pennsylvania and Georgia, there was a sudden seizure of power by the radicals in the Convention who lowered the suffrage requirement, whereas in the other states, the assumption of power had been made over a long period. Common to many was the fact that the constitutions were framed while the members of the assembly were active in

[27] Also many others not provided in the Constitution but assumed through these years, such as treaties, duties, paper money, patents (one to Longstreet in 1788 for a steam engine). *Georgia Bar Association Reports*, 1913, p. 86.

the dual capacity of constitution-makers and legislators. They were necessarily pressed for time as the documents indicate. Georgia in common with others was afraid to give the executive too long an arm; Pennsylvania and Georgia used a plural executive. Georgia and Maryland specified a minimum age for the governor. Georgia did not follow for many years the lead of Pennsylvania and Vermont in the provision for direct election of the executive, but in common with most, it gave him no veto power.

Certain omissions had to be supplied eventually. There was nothing about slavery, on which Georgia insisted in the Federal Convention of 1787; practically nothing on taxation; no restriction on special legislation. There was no mention of homestead or vested rights; of county officers or county business; of any other law than that of the State. It may be just as well that many matters such as have lengthened later Constitutions were left out. Georgia made of its first Constitution a fundamental law, not a series of acts properly belonging to the legislative branch.

## CHAPTER IV
## GEORGIA FROM 1777 TO 1789

### I. GENERAL CONDITIONS

THE period from 1777 to 1789 in Georgia history is one of many vicissitudes. It was characterized by war, shifts of the seat of government and factional disputes. Extra-constitutional functions were often assumed by the Executive Council; for example, it had, at times, to act as a sort of Red Cross for the relief of suffering. The courts were closed, anarchy and rude justice prevailed. Button Gwinnett was killed in a duel fought with Laughlan McIntosh on May 19, 1777, for making remarks that showed lack of sympathy for the Revolution; a man named Hopkins was tarred and feathered, after which he was "hoisted in a cart, illuminated for the occasion, and paraded with a crowded retinue through the principal streets of the town, four or five hours."[1] After the theater of the war was transferred to the South, one-half the property of Georgia was destroyed, its institutions were upset (slavery in particular by marauders),[2] money was scarce,[3] and there was almost comlete suspension of religious work. Some of the leading preachers in Savannah (Episcopalian and Lutheran) were Loyalists and fugitive; the church in Ebenezer was used as a stable and the one at Midway was burned. The Baptist preachers, Marshall, Bottsford, and Mercer, had been driven from the State, and the Quakers were so persecuted that they fled.[4]

There was great variation in the types of people to be found in Georgia at this time. The " elegance and culture in the few

---

[1] McCall, op. cit., II, 45.

[2] Coulter, *op. cit.*, p. 153.

[3] In 1782, Governor Martin applied to the House for relief in order to feed his family, since he had been unable to obtain his salary. Sketch in W. J. Northen, *Men of Mark in Georgia*.

[4] Smith, *op. cit.*, p. 109. However, since provision was later made for affirmation in the Constitutions, one can assume that some drifted back.

gentlemen planters, lawyers and counsellors" (for example, Few, Candler, Walton, Glasscock), contrasted with the roughness and sturdiness of men from the wilds of upper Georgia who had been flocking in during the war—men who could barely write, lived in log cabins, worked, fought the Tories at Kettle Creek, rode with Clarke and Twiggs.[5] Everywhere was desolation.[6] The Southern section was hard hit, Savannah and Augusta being in ruins. Frontier hardships were renewed in all the rural districts; perhaps typical was the home of George Mathews, who though not poor—he was possessed, among other things, of a thousand black walnut trees—lived in a one-room log cabin, the girls sleeping in the garret, and the boys in another cabin. Yet, Mathews was not unsuccessful. It would take time to rebuild the State physically, as well as to establish a sound civil government.

A visitor in Georgia shortly after the war, doubtless influenced by the weariness and hardships of travel, described the people as "the most profane, blasphemous set . . . I ever heard of." She declared that she had seen groups of fourteen to sixteen hundred assembled for public business, "and perhaps not one in fifty but what we call filthy drunk."[7] There was indeed much drinking of rum. Human life was held cheap, brutal courage set at a premium, and there was no compunction over robbery or murder of a Tory. On the other hand, there was much that was good—hospitality, chivalry, sympathy, good faith, a hatred of lying and fraud.[8]

Georgia was fertile, and its economic future was assured. In 1786 the raising of sea island cotton was begun on the coast.

---

5 Smith, *op. cit.*, p. 108.

6 John Wereat employed his Negroes and boats in 1782 to row up the Savannah River with rice to keep the people of Wilkes and Richmond Counties from starving. L. B. Evans, *History of Georgia*, p. 107. Salt was selling at two dollars a quart and a pair of shoes at twenty-five or thirty dollars. *Ibid*, p. 122.

7 *Journal of Southern History*, V, 306.

8 Smith, *op. cit.*, p. 106.

It was first exported by Alexander Bissell of St. Simon's Island.⁹ The farmers raised corn, wheat, oats, livestock, rice and tobacco. By 1800, the population of Savannah was 5,000, exports were valued at $1,750,000, and imports of dry goods, wines, tea, beef, butter, cheese, potatoes, and cider were constantly increasing.¹⁰

Long before 1800—in fact in 1781—there was published, in Philadelphia, a document signed by George Walton, William Few and Richard Howley, entitled *Observations upon the Effects of Certain Late Political Suggestions by the Delegates of Georgia*. It seems that there had been some proposal (it is not known how serious), to leave Georgia and South Carolina out of the Union. The *Observations* would do honor to a Chamber of Commerce brochure. Besides describing present exportable crops (rice, indigo, lumber, horses, tobacco, hemp, cotton, and iron ore), it listed potentialities for the future—timber for shipbuilding and bays to implement it, enough lumber to rebuild all the towns of the West Indies and enough pitch and tar for the fleets of the world. There was also included a subtle threat of danger to any union formed without these two Southern states: a time might come when they would be tempting to France or (on account of her trade with the Spanish Colonies) to England.¹¹

An examination of the Acts passed by the first legislature under the new Constitution will give some idea of the problems facing the law-makers. Some of these problems grew out of the terms of the Constitution; some stemmed from the war. Some were the result of the weaknesses of the Union; some arose from divergent ideas as to the reserved powers of government. There were acts defining treason; discouraging desertion; expelling internal enemies. One opened courts of law. One regulated pilotage. Some were to enforce collection of arrears

9 Evans, *op. cit.*, p. 139.
10 Evans, *op. cit.*, p. 154.
11 White, *Collections*, pp. 106-110.

due from persons keeping taverns, punch-houses and billiard tables, and retailers of spirituous liquors; some were to prevent gambling and horse racing. Others were to regulate and extend the trade of the State and establish an insurance office; to oblige Negro slaves to work on forts and other public works; to empower commissioners to lay out, make and repair roads and to clear the rivers; to regulate captures; to raise 66,000 pounds for governmental expenditures that might have to be made in 1777; to appoint commissioners of a land office.[12]

The British retook Savannah on December 29, 1778, after which there was practical anarchy in the State. Part of the trouble arose because, according to the phraseology of the Constitution, the terms of the governor and the legislature expired on the day before the elections of a new group. On this occasion the new legislature did not have an opportunity to meet, and in the flight from Savannah no one knew what was the constitutional status of the few members of the old government who could assemble. Consequently, two rival groups met, neither of which had any real authority, and it was a question which of the two governors and two executive councils to follow. Constitutional government was briefly restored in 1780; but when the British took Augusta and the State was practically overrun except for Richmond and Wilkes Counties, confusion again set in. Finally, in August, 1781, a legislature was elected. Who called the special elections and how they were conducted, records do not show; but after this time the State government appeared to have functioned better.[13] For the first time since the Declaration of Independence the legislative, executive and judicial powers were exercised freely. [14]

## II. Legislation

A reasonably faithful portraiture of the interests of a people may be found in its laws and in the challenges raised to them.

12 *Revolutionary Records*, I, 323.
13 *Revolutionary Records*, I, 310-411.
14 Stevens, *op. cit.*, II, 336.

Here are reflected all sorts of changes in folkways and in culture. In Georgia, the first cases of which records were published were those which came before the courts in the year 1805; in the records of that year and of later years one can find revealing portrayal of the life of the people, since all questions concerning rights of person or property were decided in the courts.

One fragment of a court record will show what importance was attached to a strict observance of the law. The fragment is from a record made in Liberty County in 1783, when the first Superior Court was held there.[15] The Court was opened " in the usual form " on Tuesday, November 18, 1783; but " on account of bad weather " a sufficient number of the officers was not present to hold court. There was an adjournment until the next day, when the same situation arose. Finally, on November 20, the Court met and the Chief Justice, George Walton, gave the following charge to the Grand Jury:

> The circuit which I have lately rode and which is now to be finished in your county, being the first since the close of the war, the best consequences may be expected to come from the good order and subordination which everywhere attended the courts, and which I doubt not will take place here. Nothing can contribute so much to confirm the blessings of peace as an invariable observance of the laws which have, or ought always to have, for their sole object the general happiness of the people.

Until 1805, as mentioned above, no court records were published; but from the laws that were passed, it is possible to find out a good deal about the interests and concerns of the people. Whether any laws were ever declared unconstitutional there is no way of knowing, but one can be reasonably sure that questions of constitutionality came up. Items taken from Marbury and Crawford's *Digest* covering the years of operation of the first Constitution 1777-1789, will prove enlightening. It was decided early (June 7, 1777), to adopt the English

15 White, *Collections*, p. 530.

law that was in force in May, 1776, in so far as it did not conflict with the Constitution of Georgia. Beyond the fundamental laws of England and the Constitution of Georgia, the field of operation of the legislature was wide. Subjects which would today be classed as national in scope came under their regulation; the rights of aliens, tables of depreciation, paper money. Many times they exercised the police power of the State, as in regulating taverns, conveyances, dams, ferries, wharves, shipping and pilotage and substitutes for militia duty, or they concerned themselves with inspection of rice, tobacco, fraud and deceit in selling beef. Sometimes matters of public morals or private conduct arose, as in prohibition of biting and gouging, regulation of types of gaming, handling of vagabonds. Besides all these, the law-makers exercised two important powers: that of taxation and that of incorporation of towns, corporations, churches and societies.

Following the provision in the Constitution for education, Richmond Academy, the oldest chartered school in Georgia, was established in 1783.[16] This was followed by free schools in other counties, Lyman Hall and Abraham Baldwin, both graduates of Yale, being leaders of the movement for education. In 1783, grants were made of a thousand acres to each county for schools and twenty thousand acres for a college. In 1784, Governor John Houstoun obtained a grant of forty thousand acres as an endowment for a college.[17] Finally, in 1785, an act "for the more full and complete establishment of a public School of Learning" was passed, inaugurating a system of centralized public education in which all public schools were to be "parts and members of the university." "It would seem . . . that the legislature, in making these provisions had in mind the establishment of an educational system like that which was later worked out in the newer states west of the Alleghanies."[18]

16 Marbury and Crawford, *op. cit.,* p. 129.
17 Evans, *op. cit.,* p. 129.
18 E. Channing, *History of the United States,* III, 568.

Abraham Baldwin [19] was chosen president of the institution. Of the need for a State University, he said:

> It shall therefore be among the first objects of those who wish well to the national prosperity to encourage and support the principles of religion and morality and early to place the youth under the forming hand of society that by instruction they may be moulded to the love of virtue and good order. Sending them abroad to other countries for their education will not answer these purposes, is too humiliating an acknowledgment of the ignorance or inferiority of your own, and will always be the cause of so great foreign attachments that upon principles of policy it is inadvisable.[20]

Actually, however, a site for the State University was not selected until later and the institution did not open until 1800. The first commencement was held in 1804, with a graduating class of nine students: Gibson Clark, Jeptha V. Harris, W. H. Jackman, James Jackson, A. S. Clayton, T. Irwin, Jared Irwin, Robert Rutherford and William Williamson.[21]

One other important series of laws was passed in this period —those concerning what were called " Head Rights." A land office was provided and a land court for each county was to be held the first Monday in each month by five justices of the peace. Every head of a family was entitled to two hundred acres for himself, and fifty acres for each member of his household —family and slaves—up to ten, provided he settle in six months. Those building a grist mill might have one hundred acres, a saw mill, five hundred acres, and a furnace or forge, two thousand acres, Revolutionary soldiers might take two hundred fifty acres tax-free for five years or two hundred

---

19 Jones, *Biographical Sketches*, pp. 7-8.

20 Baldwin, from Connecticut, a Yale University man, represented Georgia in the Federal Convention in 1787 and in local and national affairs for some years. He was a constitutionalist and a Federalist. A bachelor, he took a great deal of interest in helping worthy young men. Northen, *op. cit.*

21 White, *Statistics*, p. 73.

eighty-seven and one-half acres if they paid taxes. Continental soldiers were given two hundred thirty acres.[22]

### III. IN THE CONFEDERATION

In the meantime, in the midst of all its difficulties, Georgia was trying to cooperate with the rest of the states in supporting the Articles of Confederation, which had been framed in 1777, but not adopted until 1781. Delegates were sent to the meetings. They were not sent regularly, and sometimes, because of factional difficulties, not even officially; but on the whole, men of the best calibre in the State sat in the Congress, such men as Baldwin, Bulloch, Clay, Few, Gibbons, Gwinnett, John Habersham, John and William Houstoun, Howley, N. W. Jones, Langworthy, Pierce, Telfair, Walton, Wood, Zubly. Sometimes delegates were elected and not enough money was appropriated to pay their expenses. However, Georgia was honest in meeting requisitions made upon it for support of the war. In 1783, a fund of 103,889 pounds was established from the sale of confiscated property, the interest from which was to be used for discharging the State's obligations to the Confederation.[23] Georgia favored the idea of a strong union; in this it was actuated by the same desire for protection that had for so long kept it loyal to the union within the Empire. In assigning powers to Congress, however, the states gave over little to which they were accustomed. They had never had power to declare war, to make peace, to negotiate treaties and alliances, to regulate weights and measures or to conduct postal service. They still kept control over taxation, tariffs, tonnage and interstate commerce. Though believing in the Union, and paying as best it could its obligations, Georgia sometimes failed to respect the few powers granted to Congress. One finds it doing many things that were properly in the province of the nation—making independent treaties with the Indians,[24] setting natural-

---

[22] *Wilkes County Records*, I, p. 295.
[23] Coulter, *op. cit.*, p. 156.
[24] Details from Coulter, *op. cit.*, pp. 168-169.

ization requirements, enacting patent and copyright laws (1785) and tariff laws (1784). It had not yet developed the concept of extradition or that of giving full faith and credit to other states.

Two counties of the State seemed to think that not enough power had been granted to Congress. In 1786, a Wilkes County Grand Jury made a presentment to the effect that Congress should be given power to lay an impost of five percent on all foreign articles brought into the State. A presentment from Liberty County declared that it was a great grievance that Congress did not have power sufficient to regulate trade.[25] Since the up-country counties were apt to be Federalist in affiliation, this stand seems logical. In any case, there appears to have been no conflict in the minds of Georgians between a strong national government, "energetic and formidable," and states' rights. In spite of having, in the early days, referred to itself as "The State of Georgia by the Grace of God, free, sovereign and independent,"[26] Georgia, at the Federal Convention joined the large states in voting (save when the question of slavery came up), for a nation with far-reaching powers.

## IV. Federal Convention of 1787

When it was proposed that delegates from all the states meet together to discuss plans for strengthening the Union, Georgia readily assented.[27] It sent an able delegation consisting of Bald-

[25] Cited by Nevins, *op. cit.*, p. 418, from *N. Y. Advertiser*, January 18, 1786.

[26] Marbury and Crawford, *op. cit.* In dating Constitutions and Acts.

[27] How the State responded to the call may be judged from the commission issued to "The Honorable William Few, Esqr." (Elliott's *Debates*, I, 126-138):

> Whereas you, the said William Few are in and by an ordinance of the General Assembly of our said State, nominated and appointed a Deputy to represent the same in a convention of the United States, to be assembled at Philadelphia, for the purpose of devising and discussing all such alterations and further provisions as may be necessary to render the Federal Constitution adequate to the exigencies of the union.

win,[28] Few, W. Pierce, Walton, W. Houstoun, and Nathaniel Pendleton. The Federal Convention was held from May to September, 1787. On October 3, William Pierce sailed for home on the sloop, *Friendship,* arriving in Savannah on October 10. He brought with him a copy of the new Federal Constitution, signed in behalf of Georgia by Baldwin and Few, also a copy of the resolution passed by the Federal Convention, requesting that the Constitution be submitted to a convention of the people of each state. Three days later, a copy of the document appeared in the *Georgia State Gazette.*[29]

On October 18,[30] Governor Handley submitted the Constitution and sundry papers to the legislature. On October 25, it was resolved to make the recommendation of Congress in regard to the proposed Constitution the order of the day; on October 26 it was resolved that a convention be called at the next general election, the delegates—three from each county—to be elected in the same way as representatives to the House. The meeting was to be held in Augusta on the fourth Tuesday in December. It was resolved that any officer might be elected to the convention, and that a majority might proceed to business.

---

You are therefore hereby commissioned to proceed in the duties required of you in virtue of the said ordinance.

Witness our trusty and well-beloved George Mathews, Esq., our captain-general, governor, commander-in-chief, under his hand and our great seal, this 17th day of April in the year of our Lord, 1787, and of our Sovereignty and Independence the eleventh.

[28] Baldwin was the faithful conscientious leader of the delegation on constitutional questions. Simple, reflective, moderating in influence, he helped save the day for the great compromise. He split the vote of the delegation (as did the Maryland group), so that, in the delay caused, time was gained for compromise.

Baldwin remarked that some questions would need to be worked out later, such as separation of legislative and judicial powers, but he expressed a feeling of satisfaction that so much had been accomplished. E. S. Corwin, *Doctrine of Judicial Review,* p. 66.

[29] Albert E. Saye, *New Viewpoints in Georgia History,* pp. 222-223.

[30] House *Journal.*

GEORGIA FROM 1777 TO 1789          59

On December 25, the first meeting was held;[31] John Wereat was elected President. On Saturday, December 29, the delegates [32] proceeded to the business at hand and the Constitution was considered paragraph by paragraph. On Monday, December 31, it was unanimously resolved to adopt it; a committee consisting of Stephens, Osborne and Sullivan was appointed to prepare and report a form of deed of ratification. The form they submitted was approved by the Convention, and on Wednesday, January 2, the deed was signed. It was worded as follows:[33]

> We, the delegates of the people of the State of Georgia, in convention met . . . having taken into our serious consideration the said Constitution (agreed upon and proposed by the Deputies of the United States in General Convention held in the city of Philadelphia on the 17th day of September in the Year of Our Lord, 1787),[34] have assented to, ratified, and adopted, and by these presents do, in virtue of the powers and authority to us given by the people of the State for that

---

31 Original *Journal* in Archives Department, Atlanta, Ga.

32 There is some discrepancy in the lists of names of delegates variously given. From the White's *Collections*, p. 620, is quoted the following list:

| | | | | |
|---|---|---|---|---|
| Chatham | W. Stephens / Joseph Habersham | Richmond | W. Few / J. McNeil |
| Effingham | J. Davis / N. Brownson | | |
| Burke | E. Telfair / H. Todd | Wilkes | G. Mathews / F. Sullivan / J. King |
| Liberty | J. Powell / J. Elliott / J. Maxwell | Washington | J. Irwin / J. Rutherford |
| Glynn | G. Handley / C. Hillary / J. Milton | Greene | R. Christmas / T. Daniell / R. Middleton |
| Camden | H. Osborne / J. Seagrove / J. Weed | | |

33 Elliott's *Debates*, I, 323.

34 From the preceding paragraphs.

purpose for and in behalf of ourselves and our constituents, fully and entirely assent to, ratify and adopt the said Constitution.

Done in Convention, at Augusta, in the said State, on the 2nd day of January in the Year of Our Lord, 1788, and of the Independence of the United States the Twelfth. In witness whereof, we have hereunto subscribed our names.

> JOHN WEREAT
> President and Delegate
> from County of Richmond.

" As the last name was signed to the Ratification, a party of Colonel Armstrong's regiment quartered in the town proclaimed the joyful tidings opposite the State House by thirteen discharges from two pieces of artillery." [35] On January 5, the *Georgia Gazette* announced the unanimous ratification of the Constitution. On the same day, the Convention wound up its business by addressing a letter to the President of Congress: " We hope that the ready compliance of this State with the recommendation of Congress and the late National Convention will tend not only to consolidate the Union but promote the happiness of our common country." Habersham, King and Telfair were requested to present to the legislature the expenses of the convention. Two hundred copies of the *Journal* were to be struck off and delivered to the Executive.

Much was made of the fact that Georgia was the fourth state to ratify the Federal Constitution and that the vote for ratification was unanimous. No more than on the occasion of the enactment of the first three State Constitutions, however, was any motion made to submit the final decision to popular vote. When the question of adopting the first ten amendments to the Federal Constitution came later before the legislature, this body considered them premature, and no action was taken to ratify them. They met with the same reception in Connecticut and Massachusetts.

[35] White, *Collections*, p. 621.

Upon receipt of the report of the activities of the convention, the legislature resolved that there should be named three fit and discreet persons from each county who, as soon as possible after the ratification by nine states of the new general government, should meet in a convention to revise the State Constitution. By the sixth of October nine states had ratified, and a convention was therefore called for November. The legislature was called for the same time to decide on a method of choosing electors of President and Vice President, for the new government must be voted upon on the first Wednesday in February and must go into action on March 4, 1789.

## CHAPTER V

## THE FRAMING AND PROVISIONS OF THE SECOND CONSTITUTION

### I. THE THREE CONVENTIONS

As agreed, a Convention met in Augusta in November, 1788, to "take under consideration the alterations and amendments that are necessary to be made in the constitution of this state. . . . ."[1] that it might conform with the newly accepted general government. The twenty-seven delegates[2] appointed by the legislature assembled on November 4. They labored under the presidency of Governor George Handley for sixteen days. They kept no journal. On November 24, they presented their proposed Constitution, having exceeded the instructions given them by drafting a new document[3] rather than revising the old. Five hundred copies[4] were printed and these were submitted to the justices of the peace and militia officers. The Constitution was to be adopted or rejected by another convention, the delegates to which were to be elected on the first Tuesday

---

[1] *House Journal* 1788, pp. 155-156.

[2] One member, Nathan Brownson, deserves special note. He not only attended this first Convention and the third one which produced the accepted draft, but he had a long record of service to his credit. From the famed St. John's Parish he had gone to Yale and become a doctor. He served in the Continental Congress, was surgeon in the Continental Army, governor of the State, trustee of the University, speaker twice of the House of Representatives and had performed various other public services. (Jones, *Biographical Sketches*).

[3] In Archives of State, Atlanta.

[4] A copy of this Constitution as it was adopted after the third convention is in the New York Historical Society. It lists the following members in attendance at this first Convention: George Handley (Glynn), President; Chatham: Joseph Clay, Junior, Mathew McAllister; Effingham: N. Brownson; T. Lane; Burke: E. Telfair, G. Walton; Richmond: W. Few, J. McNiel, C. Crawford; Wilkes: A. Fort; F. Sullivan, J. King; Glynn: J. Milton, C. Hillary; Camden: H. Osborne, J. Armstrong, N. Pendleton; Washington: J. Irwin, J. Watts, J. Rutherford; Franklin: S. Gardner, N. Cleveland, M. Woods; Greene: C. Abercrombie, W. Greer, T. Houghton.

## PROVISIONS OF THE SECOND CONSTITUTION 63

in December. For this second convention three men from each county were to meet in Augusta January 4, 1789.

Twenty-seven of thirty-one members of the second Convention were members of the house. Henry Osborne presided. Again the instructions were clear, and again the meeting exceeded its authority. As a committee of the whole it considered paragraph by paragraph the Constitution submitted by the first convention, making alterations and amendments. It abolished the property qualification for voting and reduced that for the members of the house. It proposed a reduction of the terms of judges from seven to three years, and the election of the governor by a college of electors in which the counties would have equal votes. After sixteen days the delegates proposed to adjourn until the second Tuesday in June, meanwhile submitting their Constitution to the people.[5] But on February 4, 1789, the house resolved that there must be an end to meetings, and that the third convention of delegates, elected on the first Monday in April and assembling in Augusta on May 4 should be final.

William Gibbons served as president of this third Convention. Of the twenty-four members elected, only ten had served before—one evidence of the dissatisfaction felt with the second convention which had been composed so largely of members of the house. The new Convention made short shrift of the work before it, taking one day to organize, one day to consider and one day to vote, at which time it voted to adopt the Constitution as of the November before.[6] The house had given only

[5] Manuscript copy in Archives: The delegates to this Convention are listed in the copy above referred to. They were H. Osborne (Camden) president; Camden: T. Stafford; Glynn: G. Handley; Liberty: F. O'Neal, J. M'Queen; Chatham: J. Gunn, T. Gibbons, A. Emanuel; Effingham: B. Lanier, J. Green, O. Bowen; Burke: T. Lewis, D. Emanuel; Richmond: W. Stith, Junior; W. Stith, J. Wereat; Wilkes: G. Mathews, J. Williams, E. Clarke; Washington: R. Wikinson, J. Williams; Greene: A. Barnett; D. Gresham, W. Fitzpatrick; Franklin: J. Gorham, N. Cleveland, M. Woods.

[6] William Few had been a member of the first Convention. Just back from the Federal Convention where he and Abraham Baldwin had signed the Constitution of the United States for Georgia, he probably defended

one specific instruction to this Convention—to include a provision that henceforth no money should be withdrawn from public funds except by appropriation made by law. This provision has been included in all later Constitutions. On May 6, the Constitution was presented to Governor Walton in the council chamber. On receiving it, he made this reply:[7]

> Mr. President and Gentlemen of the Convention, the Constitution for the government of this state which you now deliver to me shall have the great seal affixed to it and be deposited in the office of the Secretary of State. It shall be announced to the people at large by proclamations and a sufficient number of copies printed for the use of the several counties. I hope and believe that it will be productive of public good and happiness to the objects of government and of society.

The *Georgia Gazette* on May 9, 1789, carried the following item:

> On Monday last the third convention met in the Town Hall to consider the alterations proposed by the Convention of January last to the Constitution framed by the Convention of 1788, and on Wednesday they finally adopted and ratified the new form of government, to commence in October next. The new form being an assimilation to the Federal Constitution, its ratification and deposit was announced to the town by a discharge of eleven cannons in honor of the federated states, when his Honor, with the president and members of the convention and the President and the members of the Council, repaired to the government house and drank a glass of wine to its prosperity.

---

inclusion in this Constitution of ideas similar to those in the Federal Constitution. The Journal of the Convention of 1789 shows the signers of the Constitution of May 6, 1789: W. Gibbons (Chatham) president; Chatham: A. Emanuel, J. H. Scheuber; Effingham: B. Lanier, J. Green, N. Brownson; Burke: H. Lawson, W. Little; Richmond: A. Marshall, W. F. Booker, L. Marbury: Wilkes: J. Talbot, J. Walker; Liberty: L. McIntosh; Glynn: A. Bissett; Washington: J. Irwin, J. Watts, J. Williams; Franklin: M. Woods; Greene: J. Carmichael, H. Karr.

7 Stevens, *op. cit.*, II, 390.

The Constitution of 1789 is the shortest in Georgia's history. It consists, after a brief preamble, of four articles. There is no bill of rights, nor is there any apologia such as appeared in the first Constitution. This one is obviously the work of men anxious to get the business over with quickly, in as few words as possible, their model being the Federal Constitution.

There is no statement of the division of government into three departments, but the articles are so arranged that such a division is clearly intended. Article I is concerned with the legislature, Article II with the executive, and Article III with the judiciary. Reserved for miscellaneous provisions and a few guarantees of rights is Article IV. (For purposes of convenience and clarity, some of the clauses of these Articles will in the present analysis be rearranged.) It will appear that the principle of separation of powers was again violated many times, the legislature, especially, being given regulative powers of which some properly belonged to the judiciary, some to the executive. It was not until some years later that the judges began to question this delegation of their powers.

## II. The Legislature

The major change in the legislative branch is that there were to be separate houses, a Senate and a House of Representatives, the two together being styled "the general assembly." The Senate was to be elected on the first Monday in October of every third year and was to be composed of one member from each county, elected by the electors of that county. One notes the Federal influence here: the idea of equal representation in the upper house was preserved. The qualifications for senator were that he must not be less than twenty-eight years old, and must have resided in the United States nine years, in the State three years, and in the county three months. He must own two hundred and fifty acres or have two hundred and fifty pounds in other possessions. The Senate was to elect its own president and have sole power to try impeachments, again following the Federal pattern.

The House of Representatives was to be elected annually on the first Monday in October and was to be composed of members chosen on a proportional basis; here again as in the first Constitution, the size of the electorate rather than the population was the criterion.[8] A representative must be not less than twenty-one years old, and must have resided in the United States seven years, in the State two years, in the county three months; he must own two hundred and fifty acres of land or other property to the value of one hundred and fifty pounds. The representatives were to choose their own speaker and have sole power to impeach (which seems to have been a new idea developed since 1777). The religious qualification was removed, but the provision was retained that no clergyman might sit in either house. No member of either house might hold any office or military commission (except justice of the peace or officer of the militia).

There were to be annual meetings of the General Assembly on the first Monday in November. Each house might judge its own elections, returns, and qualifications of members, and have power to expel or punish for disorderly behavior. This last is a new item, added, perhaps, on account of the rough and ready conduct which marked the times. One-third of the members of each branch might proceed to business, but a smaller number might adjourn from day to day and compel the attendance of other members.

In this Constitution was a provision reminiscent of English practice: no member was to be arrested during, or going to or from, the meetings of the General Assembly except for treason, felony or breach of the peace. A member was to have freedom

---

[8] The representation was as follows: Camden 2, Glynn 2, Liberty 4, Chatham 5, Effingham 2, Burke 4, Richmond 4, Wilkes 5, Washington 2, Greene 2, Franklin 2. It may be pointed out that in the Senate the tidewater had five seats, the middle section three and the up-country three; while in the House, the tidewater had thirteen, the middle twelve, and the up-country nine. Yet the middle and up-country sections had five times as many whites and 1¼ times as many slaves as the tidewater. Bonner, *op. cit.*, p. 96.

of debate in either house, in court, and elsewhere. As before, he must swear to be faithful in all his votes to the best interests of the State and to support the Constitution; and he must swear that he did not use bribery or other unlawful means to obtain his office. Provision was here made for affirmation (by Quakers) in the case of the legislative and executive departments.

The General Assembly was given the power of selecting a governor. The method devised is similar to that worked out in the Federal Convention, the idea being that the executive was better selected by indirect vote than by direct election. Every second year the House of Representatives, on the second day of assembling, was to choose three persons. A list was to be made of the persons voted for, for governor, with the number of votes each received. The speaker was to sign this list in the presence of the House and deliver it in person to the Senate. On the same day the Senate was to ballot, each senator voting for one of the three highest on the list submitted; a majority vote in the Senate should elect the governor. A glance at this method will indicate that the advantage here as in other votes, lay with the tidewater or with the combination of tidewater and middle section versus up-country frontier.

The General Assembly was to make all laws, and ordinances "necessary and proper," alter boundaries, make new counties,[9] and regulate their representation. It might direct the alteration of the Great Seal, point out the method of correcting errors and appeals, direct one new trial for final decision and regulate the courts-merchant. It was to establish by law the salaries of judges and of the attorney general (probably also that of the governor).[10] It might regulate and restrict the governor's appointments of militia and secretaries, and it might decide where to invest the appointment of inferior officers. In all ap-

9 Representation for counties made out of old ones should be deducted from that of the old counties. For those made out of the territory of the State representation should be regulated by the General Assembly and not exceed three persons. The question of the public land will be discussed in another connection.

10 No mention of salaries was made in the earlier Constitution.

pointments of State officers, the House should by ballot select three persons, the Senate should then, by majority vote, elect one of the three. One requirement the General Assembly must fulfill—No appropriation of public money could be made except by law.

The institution of the plural executive was abolished. The two-house Assembly dominated the governor by election and restriction of his appointive power; controlled the purse strings of the State, and regulated the activities of the judiciary. No mention is made of any compensation for their work.[11]

### III. The Executive

The governor must be at least thirty years old, a resident of the United States for twelve years, and of the State for six years. He must be possessed of five hundred acres of land within the State and of other property to the extent of a thousand pounds sterling. Again the influence of the Federal Constitution was seen in that the president of the Senate should take his place in case of death, resignation or disability. Adequately compensated, the governor was to be beholden to no other state or power. The title of Commander-in-chief of the State of Georgia and its militia was given him. In this document one notes an extension of the governor's power. He was here given the power of reprieve except in impeachment, and of pardon after conviction except for treason or murder.[12] Again, the governor might review all bills and veto any.

If the houses disagreed on adjournment, the governor might adjourn them to such time as he thought proper. He might also call extra sessions, and he must, from time to time, give the Assembly information on the state of the republic and recommend measures for passage. Two other duties he had, one

---

[11] In all cases where salary was arranged, there must be no increase or diminution during the term for which the person was elected.

[12] Even in these cases he might respite until the next General Assembly for action in pardon. However, a two-thirds vote of both houses might override his veto, and a pocket veto was arranged.

to issue writs of election in case of vacancy in the General Assembly, the other to share jointly with the Assembly the responsibility of the use of the Great Seal.

With this Constitution, then, the governor became something more than a figurehead. He was coming to be a power both in a direct and in an indirect way.

### IV. THE JUDICIARY

Still the weakest of the three departments, the judiciary got little attention. As before, a Superior Court was to be held in each county twice a year, with final decision in all cases civil or criminal except for those cases which might legally be referred to an inferior court and any that might be subject to a Federal Court.[13] Judges and attorneys-general were to hold their offices during three years. How they were chosen was not stated—one can only presume it was by the legislature. As mentioned above, it was the prerogative of the Assembly to direct one new trial, which should be final. Courts-merchant were to be held as heretofore, but no reference was made to Courts of Conscience; probably the inferior courts, conducted by the justices of peace, were to take their places. As in the old common law, jurisdiction in civil cases was to lie in the county where the defendant resided or in the county where contested land lay; in criminal cases, the trial was to be held in the courts where the crime occurred.

Although the old antagonism to the power of the governor was waning, and there was some effort in this Constitution to increase his authority, no such conclusion can be drawn in regard to the judiciary. This department lost as both the others gained. Certainly there is no evidence whatever of an intention to place the judiciary on an equal footing with either the legislative or the executive authority, and it would have been radical departure indeed to suggest what later came to be taken

---

[13] Though Georgia here admitted that there might be cases properly appealable to a Supreme Court of the nation, within a few years it became the most outspoken champion of reserved rights in dealing with the Federal Government.

for granted, the power of judicial review of acts of the legislature.

## V. Miscellaneous

Of miscellaneous provisions there were eight. The electorate for the Assembly must be citizens at least twenty-one years of age who had resided in the State and in the county for six months and had paid their taxes for the preceding year. All elections were to be by ballot.[14] Freedom of the press and of religion were provided, and trial by jury and *habeas corpus* reaffirmed. Estates could not be entailed, and the widow of an intestate had her choice between sharing equally with all the children and taking her dower. If there were no widow, then an equal division shoud be made between the children and their legal representatives of the first degree. The distribution of the property of intestates not leaving widow or child was to be by law.

The Constitution was to go into effect on the first Monday in October. The executive might advance the sittings of superior courts so that elections in the counties might be expedited.

Realizing that changes would be needed in the future, the delegates provided that in 1794 three men from each county should be elected for a new convention, the time of which should be fixed by the General Assembly. Any alterations thought necessary were to be considered. If two-thirds of the whole number of delegates agreed to proceed to alter and amend, a majority was to determine the specific changes to be made.

Before the meeting thus arranged could assemble, very stirring events had taken place in Georgia which split the State. The convention was held; but attention was centered on other matters, and only a few recommendations for change were made. A plan was laid, however, for a later convention. Presumably this would give an opportunity for passions to cool and a more judicious frame of mind to assert itself.

14 The provisions have been described in other connections.

## CHAPTER VI
## GEORGIA FROM 1789 TO 1798

### I. GEORGIA AND THE NATION

DURING the few years following 1793 occurred the conflict with the national government in which Georgia objected to review by the Supreme Court of its legislative acts. Its championship of states' rights became pronounced. In the case of Chisholm v. Georgia [1] lengthy opinions were rendered not only on the right of a citizen of one state to sue another state, but also on the nature of the Union. The Federal Constitution provided that the judicial power of the United States should extend to controversies " between a state and citizens of another state;" it was therefore competent for the Supreme Court to rule upon the case. The decision was against Georgia, and it was ordered to pay the debt claimed. It refused and threatened death " without benefit of clergy " to anyone who tried to collect. On the nature of the union, Justice Wilson, supported by Chief Justice Jay, said that the people of the nation had retained sovereignty and had not granted it to the states—the people had established a Constitution by which state governments should be bound. Georgia protested violently. It was not alone in its stand for states' rights. Maryland, New York, and Massachusetts shortly followed.[2] The eleventh amendment to the Federal Constitution, 1794, ratified 1798,[3] later vindicated

---

[1] 2 Dallas 419 (1793).

[2] A. C. McLaughlin, *A Constitutional History of the United States*, p. 302.

[3] " Georgia in her early history was the most obstreperous litigant over whom the Supreme Court had original jurisdiction. Her resistance to its mandates led to the passage of the eleventh amendment, and her unconstitutional legislation first called into exercise the great powers of the Court announced in Fletcher *v.* Peck (6 Cranch 87). Despite her recalcitrant behavior she has had the honor of contributing to the Supreme Court Bench three members, Wayne, Campbell and Lamar " (*Georgia Bar Association Reports* (1894) p. 149). Campbell however, served from Alabama. The case of Fletcher *v.* Peck occurred in 1810, followed by two other contests, the Cherokee Nation *v.* Georgia (5 Peters 115) (1831) and Worcester *v.* Georgia (6 Peters 515) (1832).

Georgia's position.

## II. LOCAL INTERESTS

In the absence of court records, a barometer of thought and action in any period may be found in the acts of the legislature. For the first time since 1782, an act was passed (in 1795) governing the admission of attorneys.[4] Other acts passed during the period from 1789 to 1798 dealt with transportation, roads, bridges, canals, communication via marshes, navigation of rivers, wharves, shipping and pilotage, state carriages, ferries, lighthouses. Others incorporated the Savannah merchants

---

In the case of the Bank of the United States *v.* Deveaux (6 Cranch 61) (1810), "it was because of a denial by the Supreme Court of Federal jurisdiction . . . that the fundamental construction of the Constitution in McCulloch *v.* Maryland (1819) was not announced nine years earlier. The court held (afterwards reversed) that a corporation was not a citizen of another state within the constitutional jurisdiction of 'controversies between citizens of the foreign state'." This caused the dismissal of a suit by a United States bank against a Georgia sheriff who had seized $2,005.00 of the bank's money in collection of taxes (*Georgia Historical Quarterly*, VII (1923) pp. 300-301).

[4] Prior to the code of 1863 there was no method for examination. The candidate's moral rectitude was certified to the judge of the Superior Court, after which he took an approved examination in open court. By the code of 1863 the candidate must be a citizen, of good moral character; he must have read the law in the circuit and must prove that he had done so by statements of two attorneys or other satisfactory evidence. His examination was to be in (1) common and statute law of England of force in the State, (2) law of pleading and evidence, (3) principles of equity, (4) revised code, Constitution of the Confederate States and this State, rules of Practice of the Superior Courts. The code of 1868 substituted the Constitution of the United States for the Confederate one. In 1897 the examination required became a written one, prepared by the Supreme Court, conducted under supervision of the Judges of the Superior Courts. The name of the applicant was not to be disclosed until after the examination. This statute went into effect on August 1, 1868, but no one was admitted under it. In 1898 an Amendment provided that the judges of the Supreme Court might appoint a board of three examiners to conduct a written examination. Two practising attorneys must certify to the good character of the candidates. These rules did not apply to diploma holding candidates, the graduates of the Lumpkin Law School being admitted without examination after 1859, Mercer after 1875, of Emory University after 1888 and of Atlanta Law School after 1893. *Georgia Bar Association Reports* (1899-1900), pp. 118-131.

(1793), the Augusta Mechanical (1794), the Grand Lodge of Georgia Masons (1794), the Fire Company of Savannah and Augusta (1794). Many land acts were passed, some for ordinary citizens, others for the late troops. There was an act to punish forgery, another to punish horse stealing (1793), one on marks and brands (1792), one on quarantine, and one licensing peddlers.

Taxation, then as always, assumed large proportions. Laws for the inspection of tobacco, lumber and slaves were passed; also an act for licensing taverns (1791). Rights of citizenship were restored to those who had been deprived of them during the Revolution by the confiscation and amercement acts. Much time was spent in granting divorces.[5] Estates of orphans were protected and provision was made for the poor (1792). In 1796 an act was passed to enable executors to manumit slaves.[6]

Life was not so complex then, and one may presume, for want of record, that justice was found at the hands of the local or Superior Courts. If a law were challenged, appeal could be made to the judge when he came on circuit. Sometimes, to be sure, recourse was had to the " field of honor " and sometimes to a rough and ready decision.

### III. Yazoo Fraud

Shortly before the time arrived for the calling of the convention for alterations in the Constitution of 1789, an event occurred which split Georgia and paved the way for friction both internal and national for years. It was this period which witnessed the Yazoo scandal. In 1789 four stock companies were formed to sponsor the sale and settlement of Georgia's western lands. The companies did not comply with the agreement with the legislature, and the sales were not completed. In 1789 new companies were formed, one of which was the famous Yazoo Company. Governor Mathews vetoed the bill, but in

5 See Discussion of Constitution of 1798 for this subject.
6 This subject was enlarged and defined in the Constitution of 1798.

1795 it was passed again and the governor signed it.[7] Thirty-five million acres of land claimed by Georgia were sold by the legislature for $500,000. With one exception, every member of the legislature who voted for the measure got a share.[8] When the people got word of what had happened, they were aroused; cries of bribery rang throughout the State. The intrepid James Jackson, famous duellist, fiery in the cause of right, resigned his seat in the Senate to come home and denounce the fraud.[9]

Constitutionally the case is interesting from two points of view. First, it was another in a series of contests which took place in the early years between Georgia and the Federal Supreme Court. The issue in this instance was whether a legislature may void the acts of a previous legislature and rescind a grant which has once been made. The answer was no.[10]

[7] George Mathews, a native of Virginia, had been an Indian fighter, a revolutionary figure serving with Washington and Greene. He had removed to Georgia in 1785, establishing his home in the Goose Pond region on Broad River, where he persuaded others to join him. An independent in his thinking (he was, for one thing, a phonetic speller) and in his course of action, this interesting figure in his "knee breeches, fair-topped boots, shirt ruffled at bosom and wrists, and sword dangling" (Northen, *Men of Mark*, I, 226-234), illiterate, upright, believed that the sovereign power of the State lay in the legislature, and did not believe a governor's veto in the public land case justified.

[8] Coulter, *op. cit.*, pp. 186-192.

[9] In 1796 the legislature met for the first time at Louisville and Jackson introduced a Rescinding Act which was passed by both houses and signed by Governor Irwin on February 13, 1796. The act of sale was voided and arrangements were made to pay back the money to the companies. There was an impressive scene when the papers were taken out into the open and set afire by the reflection of the sun on a piece of glass. The companies took their case to the Federal Supreme Court. Meanwhile Georgia had ceded the land to the United States in 1802. At the same time the Federal government ceded Georgia a twelve mile strip in the north making the 35th parallel the State boundary line. (L. L. Knight, *Bicentennial Memoirs*, p. 161). The Supreme Court decided that the claims were valid and that a State is bound by the obligation of contract as individuals are. The decision in the Yazoo Case was not rendered until 1810. (Fletcher *v.* Peck, 6 Cranch 87).

[10] Though the affair took its title from the Yazoo Company and the famous Supreme Court case of Fletcher *v.* Peck involved this company,

Second, the publicity given to the Yazoo sale and the demand for the sale's rescission had its effect upon the work of the Constitutional Convention of 1795.

## IV. CONVENTION OF 1795

The meeting [11] assembled in May 1795, had as president a man long prominent in the State—Noble W. Jones. London-born, Savannah-reared, doctor and farmer, Jones had served as Speaker of the Commons House in colonial days, and had taken a strong stand against the king. He had served in the war in the Continental Congress, and in the State Assembly[12]

A Rules Committee reported suggestions: that an oath of loyalty to the Constitution of the United States be taken; that one penny per minute be charged for tardiness of more than fifteen minutes after the president had taken the chair, unless for reasonable excuse; that there be no conversing during business, and no unbecoming language; that no one be permitted to speak more than three times on a matter without leave; that there be a two-dollar fine for refractory conduct; that no unfair construction be put on debate; that motions be made in writing if required by the president; that no one be allowed to pass between the chairs in the course of a speech; that members be required to retain their seats until the president should leave the room.

It was perhaps expected that the delegates would present comprehensive alterations. They evidently felt, however, that

---

there was an equally important case in connection with another of the companies, found in a little volume entitled *The Case of the Georgia Sales on the Mississippi Considered* (with a reference to Law Authorities and Public Acts). The contention in this case was that the legislature in repealing the act for the sale of lands was assuming judicial functions; if this were to be permitted, what became of the system of checks and balances? R. G. Harper, Philadelphia, Richard Folwell, 1799.

11 *Journal of the Convention of 1795.*

12 Jones helped welcome George Washington to Georgia in 1791. At the time of his death in 1805 he was serving as president of the Georgia Medical Society.

the time was not ripe—there was too much excitement and bandying of charges over the Yazoo situation. They heard petitions for freer rule of public lands, made a few amendments, and provided for a later convention (which was called for May, 1798), presumably hoping that feelings would have quieted down by that time. They spent most of their time on questions of representation. In the period 1790-1795 seven new counties had been added—three in the up-country, in newly settled territory; two in the middle section; two in the tidewater, where new counties were carved out of old ones so that the old ratio between the tidewater and the other sections might be maintained.[13] Not to be outdone, the upper section, by a very close vote (29-26), succeeded in having apportionment based upon county population. Thus the lower counties got twenty-five representatives, the upper twenty-six. All voting by the General Assembly was to be by joint ballot, another slight edge being thus given to frontier sections. Annual election of senators was provided. Louisville was made the seat of government.

The time of meeting of the General Assembly was changed to January without any provision being made for a government to function between November, when the existing government expired, and that date. Presumably Georgia was without an official government for two months. It speaks well that in spite of the bitterness of the Yazoo affair it could be said:

> A more inflammable or less law-abiding people would in these two months, under the influences then at work, have set in motion, if not carried to completion, agencies which would have over-turned the government and given up the state to anarchy and misrule.[14]

One clause that never appeared before, is significant—" All powers not delegated by the constitution, as amended, are retained by the people."

13 Bonner, *op. cit.*, p. 97.
14 Stevens, *op. cit.*, II, 409.

## CHAPTER VII

## HOW THE CONSTITUTION OF 1798 WAS CONSTRUCTED

### I. The Convention

THE Constitutional Convention of 1798, held for the purpose of considering any further alterations and amendments that might be necessary, exceeded its authority and submitted a new Constitution. Though the people never ratified it, they received it, when it was proclaimed to them, " with peculiar joy." [1]

Fifty-six delegates from twenty-one counties met on May eighth.[2] By the tenth, two more counties were represented. That Jared Irwin should preside was natural in view of his experience in the Conventions of 1789 and 1795. On Friday, May eleventh, the meeting was turned into a committee of the whole; and so it functioned with James Powell as chairman, until May thirtieth. Day by day, provisions of the Constitution were discussed, then referred to committees. After being reported to the committee of the whole, the measures were then acted upon formally by the Convention. A few men took the lead in the convention, each framing or being responsible for one or more measures.[3] In the library of the New York Historical Society there is a copy of the *Constitution of the State of Georgia as Revised Amended and Compiled by the Convention of the State at Louisville on the Thirtieth Day of May 1798*. This copy is inscribed " George Jones, Esquire." Along the margin, in the same handwriting, are the names of the

---

[1] Stevens, *op. cit.*, II, 500.

[2] It would be impossible to sketch here all the members of the Convention. One of the most interesting was Thomas J. Spalding, for whom Spalding County was later named. He proved to be the last surviving member of the convention. He had a long and useful career. He was the author of a life of Oglethorpe, and of sketches and articles published in agricultural journals. He was one of the earliest cotton planters in the State, and he introduced into Georgia the manufacture of sugar cane. White, *Collections*, p. 636.

[3] *Record of the Convention of 1798*.

gentlemen who framed the various sections.[4] The names of three members from Chatham County occur frequently: James Jones contributed the section on powers of the Executive; George Jones those on freedom of the press, trial by jury, honesty in office, security for honest debtors, and the promotion of the advancement of the arts and sciences; Major General James Jackson (also Governor) devised the sections on western lands,[5] territorial boundaries and the Judiciary.[6] Notable contributions were made by others. Peter Carnes offered the article against further importation of slaves, Jesse Mercer the one on liberty of conscience,[7] Robert Watkins the one deal-

[4] Article I: (1) James Jones, (3) 1795, (11) J. Jones, (13) J. Jones, (15) George Jones, (16) J. Jones, (17) George Jones, (18) Watkins, (19) J. Jones, (20) Cochran, (21) Taliaferro, (23) Jackson, (24) Jackson.
Article II: (1) J. Jones, (2) J. Jones, (6) J. Jones, (9) Taliaferro, (11) George Jones, (12) J. Jones, (13) J. Jones, (14) Taliaferro.
Article III: (1) Jackson, (2) J. Jones, (3) J. Jones, (4) J. Jones, (5) Watkins, (6) Stith, (7) Taliaferro, (8) Fouche, (9) Jackson, (10) J. Jones, (11) J. Jones.
Article IV: (1) partly by Barnett, . . . from "provided" on by Jackson, (2) Taliaferro, (3) J. Jones, (4) Taliaferro, (5) George Jones, (6) George Jones, (7) George Jones, (8) Jackson, (9) J. Jones (10) Jesse Mercer, (11) Carver, (12) Stith, (13) George Jones, (14) Watkins.
The paragraph "we, the underwritten delegates . . ." J. Jones.

[5] He, it will be recalled, had taken the lead in rescinding the fraudulent Yazoo Act.

[6] T. U. P. Charlton in his *Life of Major-General James Jackson* (1809) credits Jackson with much if not the greater part of the Constitution of 1798. Jackson was an outstanding leader of the period — English-born, Revolutionary fighter, student of law under George Walton, state legislator, congressman, senator, governor. The portrait found in Northen, *op. cit.,* I, shows him slender, long-nosed, thin-jawed, his straight hair tied back, his shirt beruffled at neck and cuff. With his intensely blue eyes, quick temper, fine quality of mind and character, he was appreciated by Bulloch, Habersham, Houstoun, Jones and Hall. He was a strong defender of human liberty.

[7] It had been moved by a lawyer that ministers of the gospel be ineligible to the office of legislator. This was advocated by doctors and lawyers. When Mr. Mercer offered an amendment that both these professions be included in the restriction, the measure was quickly dropped.

CONSTITUTION OF 1798 WAS CONSTRUCTED 79

ing with election frauds. James Fouche should be credited with the section providing for the first time for a digest of the laws.[8]

A complete file for 1798 of the *Columbian Museum and Savannah Advertiser* contains no reference to this Constitution except that its complete text was published on July 3. Occupying the second page and one and one-half columns of the third page, it appeared with no editorial comment whatever.[9] Much more concern was felt about the rise of the consulate in France.

## II. THE CONSTITUTION ITSELF

The Constitution of 1798 was a great improvement over its predecessors. Its main defect is that it lengthened the Constitution and included many things properly belonging in a code of laws. However, if one judges a Constitution's success by the length of time it served and the number of amendments necessary, this one must have been singularly successful. Georgia did not again form a Constitution until 1861.[10] It amended this Constitution only twenty-three times. During the years that it functioned, Georgia participated in the great political and socioeconomic changes in the country.[11]

The changes made by the amendments seem to reflect the era of Jacksonian democracy. The election of justices of the

[8] This will be discussed in the analysis of the Constitution of 1798.

[9] General Gunn of Camden and Colonel Thomas Glascock of Richmond declined to sign, since they claimed that under Section 23 of Article I the State was depriving them of land which they held under the Yazoo Act of 1795. The signing of the Constitution which took place on May 30, 1798, was announced to the public by sixteen rounds of artillery. Neither the convention nor the Constitution received much attention in the newspapers.

[10] The Constitutions of 1798 and 1877 were the only ones Georgia has had which were formed under peaceful conditions, and they were the longest-lived, that of 1798 lasting 63 years, that of 1877, 68 years. The Constitutions of 1777, 1861, and 1945 were war instruments, those of 1789, 1865, and 1868 were reconstruction documents.

[11] Jeffersonian revolution, era of hard feeling, era of good feeling, Mexican War, Compromise of 1850, development of industry, transportation. See Chapter IX.

peace was given to the people in 1819, that of the governor in 1824. Granting of divorce was taken from the legislature and assigned to two special juries in 1833, thus lightening the pressure of work upon the legislators. The year 1835 witnessed two important changes: the property qualification for senators and representatives was dropped and a Supreme Court was established with judges subject to removal. A few years later, in 1847, the property qualification for governor was also removed. The year 1855-1856 saw limitations placed on grants by the legislature of corporate power and the removal of some powers into the hands of the inferior courts.

How this Constitution worked becomes clear as one studies the records of the courts shortly after it was passed, and sees how any infringement of personal rights or any disregard of legislative acts was challenged. In the light of the test cases before the courts and the decisions upon them one is able to view the whole period in panorama.[12]

In this Constitution there was no preamble and no Bill of Rights, but the four articles followed the same pattern as that of the Constitution of 1789. There was a distinct separation of powers into three departments. A two-house form of General Assembly was to be elected annually.[13] The old property qualifications for holding office were maintained; to these was added the condition that the candidate must have an estate competent

[12] See Chapter VIII.

[13] The meetings were made biennial by an amendment made in 1843 and annual again by one made in 1857; they were to be held in November—for not more than forty days unless by special vote.

By the Act of 1843 the Senate was to consist of not over 47 members, one elected from each senatorial district. (The grouping of contiguous counties into senatorial districts was to be made by the General Assembly adopting the amendment.) In 1852 biennial sessions were to begin, and from that time on the Senate was to consist of one senator from each county. The house was to be composed of one hundred thirty members, each county having one representative, no county more than two. Appointment to the house was to be made by the General Assembly adopting the amendment and changed if necessary after each subsequent enumeration of inhabitants.

## CONSTITUTION OF 1798 WAS CONSTRUCTED 81

to discharge his just debts.[14] He must not hold office until all public money held by him was accounted for. Equal representation in the senate was maintained, but in the house the counties were to be represented according to an enumeration of population by census every seven years.[15] There were to be two members for every three thousand persons, three members for every seven thousand, four members for every twelve thousand, every county, however, having at least one representative and not more than four. Five persons of color were to count only as much as three whites.[16]

The power of trying impeachment was better defined in this Constitution than in previous ones. A vote of two-thirds of the members present was necessary to convict, and judgment was not to extend further than removal from office and disqualification for holding office.[17]

As a result of the land troubles, provision was made for fixing the boundaries of present and future counties. The boundaries of the State were carefully defined, including the temporary line and all land and water within jurisdictional rights and islands within twenty leagues of the coast, as well as the lands beyond the temporary line which were the "property of the free citizens of this State and held by them in sovereignty,"

[14] Three of the twenty-three amendments to this Constitution bore on qualifications for senator, representative and governor: On December 19, 1835, the property qualifications for senator and representative were removed completely, and by an amendment of December 30, 1847, those for governor were similarly dropped.

[15] The census was to be made (with remuneration) by persons appointed by ten justices of ten Inferior Courts.

[16] In the senate, according to this arrangement, control was given to the planters; here the lower counties gained a little advantage. In the house, the up-country won an edge, getting thirty-one representatives compared with a combined voting strength of tidewater and middle section of only twenty-seven. (Bonner, *op. cit.*, p. 98.)

[17] The party afterwards, of course, was subject to indictment and trial. This clause was probably enlarged in the light of the recent Yazoo fraud, as was the rule that no one might sit in either house or hold any office until all public money held by him had been accounted for.

"inalienable but by their consent." The only proviso to this was that a sale or contract with the United States might be made. But:

> Monopolies of land by individuals being contrary to the spirit of our free government, no sale of territory of this state, or any part thereof, shall take place to individuals or private companies, unless a county or counties shall have been first laid off, including such territory, and the Indian rights shall have been extinguished thereto.[18]

The Yazoo fraud caused the provision that money paid for the original purchases of the disputed land would be refunded, but not for land purchased after the Rescinding Act of 1796 or the appropriation laws of 1796 and 1797. Protection to the State Treasury followed in two clauses: first, that "no money shall be drawn out of the Treasury or from the public funds of this State, except by appropriations made by law," and second, "no vote, resolution, law or order shall pass the general assembly granting a donation or gratuity in favor of any person whatever but by the concurrence of two-thirds of the general assembly." [19] As one historian has said, " Georgia was the forerunner by a half century in the field of abolition of special pleading." [20]

Enlargement of other sections might be noted. One judges that conduct in the legislative bodies had not been above reproach since the power was given to each house not only to determine its rules, but to expel or punish "by censuring, fining, imprisoning, or either" for disorderly behavior. It might expel anyone convicted of felony or other infamous offence. It might also punish by imprisonment during session any citizen who might be guilty of disrespect or of disorderly or contemptuous behavior in its presence or who might "threaten harm to the body or estate of any mem-

---

18 Article I, Section 23.
19 *Ibid*, Section 24.
20 *Georgia Bar Association Reports*, 1921, p. 293.

ber," or who might assault or arrest any member going to or from a meeting, or rescue anyone who had been arrested by either house. Another section specified ten days before and ten days after a session during which a member might be free from arrest except for treason, felony or breach of the peace. He might be held to answer, not for what he said in debate, but for perjury, bribery or corruption. Each member of the General Assembly must swear or affirm that he had not obtained his election by bribe, threat or canvassing for election, and that he considered himself " constitutionally qualified."

For the first time it was provided that each house should keep a journal, and record the vote on any issue if two members so wished. For the first time, too, the lower house was given the right to initiate all bills for raising revenue. A clause which furnished the basis of many a case later before the courts, and which is supposed to be the first statement of its kind in the country,[21] is the proviso that no law or ordinance might pass containing any matter different from that expressed in the title, a protection against riders to bills. Every bill must be read in each branch three times, on three separate days ("unless in cases of actual invasion or insurrection ").

Though, by this Constitution, the General Assembly might make all laws " necessary and proper," great care to safeguard the rights of the people is evident. The legislature's powers are more specifically defined than before. Public money was more carefully protected and eligibility for office was hedged in. For the purpose of restricting the legislature and of saving time for other matters, certain kinds of duties and powers were taken out of its hands by an amendment passed by Acts of 1855-56, stating that:

> The Legislature shall have no power to grant corporate powers and privileges, except to Banking, Telegraph and Railroad Companies, nor to change names, nor to legitimate persons, nor to make or change precincts, nor to establish bridges

[21] *Georgia Bar Association Reports,* 1921, p. 284.

or ferries, but shall by law prescribe the manner in which said power shall be exercised by the Superior or Inferior Courts, and the privileges to be enjoyed.

Other evidences of curtailment will appear as the various articles and section are analyzed.

There were no startling changes, extensions or retractions in the position of the executive. The governor was still to be selected by the General Assembly, though the method was not specified.[22] The property qualification was retained (until 1847), and other powers and privileges remained the same. There was, however, a specific statement that the governor might appoint his own secretaries, and provision was made for a secretary of State, a treasurer, and a surveyor-general.

The great seal was to be kept by the secretary of state and used only by the governor or the General Assembly. A new one was to be devised and adopted however, after the convention.[23]

The sections on the judiciary and the amendments to these sections made from time to time, represent a great increase in the attention paid to this department. Many of the framers were lawyers. Eleven sections of the Constitution and eight of the twenty-three amendments dealt with the courts. The Court-mer-

[22] By an Act of 1824 the governor for the first time was elected by the people. The returns were to be opened in a joint meeting of the houses. If no one received a majority, the General Assembly should vote by joint ballot between the two highest.

[23] In 1799 the permanent seal of Georgia was devised. It consisted of a round disk about two inches in diameter. On one side are three pillars representing the three departments of the government supporting the arch Constitution, the pillars being inscribed with the words "Wisdom", "Justice", "Moderation". Near the pillar marked "Moderation" is a man with a drawn sword representing the military defense of the State. The inscription says "State of Georgia 1799". On the other side is a scene representing the seashore with ships flying the United States flag riding at anchor near the wharf where are hogsheads of tobacco, and bales of cotton. A little boat is landing hogsheads and boxes. In the background is a man ploughing and a flock of sheep under a flourishing tree. The inscription says "Agriculture and Commerce 1799".

## CONSTITUTION OF 1798 WAS CONSTRUCTED 85

chant was finally dropped, as had been the Court of Conscience previously. The Inferior Courts assumed all civil cases, subject to appeal to the Superior Courts. Their justices were to be appointed by the legislature, and subject to recall.[24] The inferior courts were to name justices of the peace responsible for trying cases in which not more than thirty dollars was involved, and were to have power of ordinary. A clerk was to keep the records, and issue citations, temporary letters, and marriage licenses.

The jurisdiction of The Superior Courts, whose judges were elected for three years was clarified: final and exclusive in all criminal and land cases; appellate or concurrent in all others, with full power to correct errors in the proceedings of Inferior Courts.[25]

The office of sheriff was highly considered in those days. Here the first official provision was made for this position. They were to be appointed for two years, subject to recall, but might hold office only two out of four years.

A rider, which might indicate a move for a short ballot, was attached to the section on the sheriffs. It stated that no county officer might be elected on the day of the election of members of the General Assembly.

A forward-looking provision of the Constitution of 1798 was that " within five years after the adoption of this consti-

---

24 The recall principle was applicable to all the members of the judiciary. Georgia took the lead in this progressive movement.

By an amendatory act of 1812 the justices of the Inferior Courts were to be elected every fourth year, as were the justices of the peace. Forthcoming elections must be advertised in public places.

25 Some changes took place, over the years, in the judiciary. In 1819 the election of inferior court justices was given to the people. Prior to 1836, terms of judges of the Superior Courts extended from three to four years. By constitutional amendment in 1843, action was taken on the amendment of 1835, for establishing the Supreme Court of three judges elected by the general assembly for six years. In 1852 another amendment gave the election of judges to the respective circuits of the State. In 1858 the legislature voluntarily gave a ruling of the Superior Court the position of a law of the State. (*Georgia Bar Association Reports*, 1909. J. R. Lamar, *History of Establishment of Supreme Court of Georgia*, p. 103).

tution, the body of our laws, civil and criminal, shall be revised, digested and arranged under proper heads and promulgated in such manner as the legislature may direct . . ."[26]

The legislature was curbed and the activities of the judiciary increased in the provision in regard to divorces. Hitherto, divorces had been granted by the legislature. Though the num-

[26] George and Robert Watkins framed the earliest compilation of Georgia statutes. Since it contained the Yazoo Act as well as the Rescinding Act Governor Jackson opposed it. The legislature never adopted the code, though a small appropriation was later voted to defray the expenses. (Knight, *Bicentennial Memoirs,* p. 160). The history of the code of Georgia is in three periods: compilation, digest, and, finally, code. In the first period the work of Marbury and Crawford appeared (1802), called a digest, but really only a compilation to 1800. An act of 1809 provided that during 1810 all the laws and resolutions passed since 1800 be compiled and that this be done every tenth year thereafter. Under this act, three compilations were made: that of A. S. Clayton, 1800-1810; L. Q. C. Lamar 1810-1819, and W. H. Dawson 1819-1829. These compilations included all laws and resolutions whether in force or not, whether public, general, private or local. (*Georgia Bar Association Reports,* 1899, p. 67). In 1819 an act was passed calling for a "Digest or Manual of the laws of Georgia" to be made during 1820, "including all acts and resolutions of the Legislature heretofore passed and which may be passed during the present session public and general, excluding private and local and such as have been repealed." This digest was to be made independently of the Act of 1809. Under this later act Oliver H. Prince was commissioned to make the digest. He submitted one in 1821. It was approved by the governor in 1822.

In 1837 Prince published a second edition, including the Dawson compilation and all statutes in force to December 1837, and in 1851 T. R. R. Cobb brought the work down to the year 1851.

By an act of 1858 the third period of codification was reached. Three commissioners were to prepare a code of all the laws of Georgia from common law, Constitutions, statutes, decisions of the Supreme Court or statutes of England in force in Georgia. The commissioners selected were David Irwin, T. R. R. Cobb and Richard H. Clark. Judge Clark stated (*Memoirs of Judge Richard H. Clark,* ed. Lollie Belle Wylie, p. 391) that the author of the scheme of the code was George A. Gordon of Savannah, but that it was executed by each of the three working independently on sections, and together on the whole. It was adopted in 1860. Judge Clark gave credit to Georgia for its leadership in judicial reform. [He tried to locate the author of the Act of 1798 by which Georgia gave up special pleading. He credited the judiciary Act of 1799 to Judge Stith or to Abraham Baldwin. In 1852 Georgia led again in drawing up the *Forms for Pleading* (author John A. Jones). (*Memoirs,* pp. 388-392.)]

## CONSTITUTION OF 1798 WAS CONSTRUCTED 87

ber was not large [27] this seemed an overlapping of the functions of the departments. Henceforth, divorces were to be granted by the legislature only after the parties had had a fair trial before the Superior Court.[28] Though the judges should try the cases,[29] the legislature still wanted the last word.

Some miscellaneous provisions are worthy of attention: care was taken to provide that " in case of an invasion and the inhabitants shall be driven from any county," elections should be held in the nearest county " not in a state of alarm " without having paid the tax required of electors. Another novelty of this Constitution was the method of voting in the General Assembly. All elections were to be by joint ballot.[30] In all elec-

---

[27] 291 persons were divorced in the period 1798-1835. (*Georgia Bar Association Reports,* 1906, p. 144). In 1902-1905, 161 cases per year were tried in Fulton County alone, as compared with 28 cases per year for the whole State in the period 1830-1835.

[28] Only partial divorce had been obtainable down to 1784. From then to 1850 the common law was used in cases of total divorce. (*Georgia Bar Association Reports,* 1906, pp. 141-142.) By Act of 1833, divorces became final after the parties obtained two concurrent verdicts of two special juries. In 1849 this was amended by adding " authorizing a divorce upon such legal principles as the general assembly may by law prescribe," to give discretionary rights whereas heretofore only ecclesiastical principles had been used. (McElreath, *op. cit.*, p. 107.)

[29] Confidence in the judges was increasing. Georgia's native bar, at this time, was small but good, college graduates of Yale, Princeton, and the Litchfield Law School. (C. Warren, *History of the Harvard Law School* I, pp. 115-116). Georgia sent more students to the latter institution than any state outside New England and New York. In the years 1798-1817 thirty-five attended as compared with seventy-two from Massachusetts, forty-four from New York, and twenty-seven from South Carolina. In the years 1817-1833, New York sent eighty-one, Georgia twenty-nine, Pennsylvania twenty-one. (*Ibid,* p. 181). Stephen F. Miller mentions thirty-three lawyers in his *Bench and Bar of Georgia,* ten of whom were educated in eastern law schools and attained national prominence. (Baldwin (Yale); Berrien, Wayne, Forsyth, Early, Colquitt (Princeton); Lamar, Dawson, Foster, Rutherford (Litchfield). The earlier group, those of the mid-eighteenth century, of which George Walton is the outstanding example, probably worked under the influence of the English barristers who practiced in Savannah.

[30] This would increase the voting strength of the up-country, thus removing some of the advantages gained by the planters of the tidewater in the Senate.

tions by the people, the voting was to be done *viva voce*.[31]

In this miscellaneous section one finds reaffirmed protection of individual rights: trial by jury; *habeas corpus* ("unless in case of rebellion or invasion the public safety should require its suspension."); *ex post facto;* freedom of press; and the right to plead one's cause. A fine statement on religious freedom appeared in this Constitution, similar to the Virginia Act for establishing religious freedom. It protected a person in his privilege of worshipping God agreeably to his conscience without taxation or maintenance and without jeopardy to his civil rights.

In this article, too, one notes the first statement in a Georgia Constitution in regard to debtors.[32] It said: "where there is not a strong presumption of fraud," the person of a debtor "shall not be detained in prison after delivering up, *bona fide*, all his estate for his creditors, as regulated by law."[33]

For the first time, one will note Georgia's taking official recognition of slaves by name in a Constitution. There was to be no future importation of slaves from Africa or any foreign

[31] Perhaps this was to enable those who could not read and write to participate.

[32] The subject had been the basis for previous acts: An Act of 1766 had provided for alleviation for imprisonment for debt and relief of debtors in jail and unable to support themselves. They could surrender whatever property they had on oath, the creditor then being able to detain them but required to pay their support. If a debtor's trade could be carried on in prison, he could support himself.

[33] In 1822 a small exemption was allowed. In 1823 he was allowed to give bond, in 1834 to exempt the family Bible. In 1835 the benefit of exemptions was extended to the debtor's family; in 1841 the exemptions might include some land, a horse and some hogs (exemptions increased 1843, 1845). In an act of 1847 no widow or other single woman was to be arrested or imprisoned for debt. According to this act, the wife was not exempted from imprisonment for debt. If the debt was joint, husband and wife were jailed together. (Smith *v.* Taylor and Wife, 2 Georgia *Reports* 22). In 1858 the final move was made to abolish imprisonment for debt on certain conditions and in 1868 came the final "there shall be no imprisonment for debt."

## CONSTITUTION OF 1798 WAS CONSTRUCTED 89

place after October 1, 1798.[34] The legislature was to have no power to prevent emigrants from any other states from bringing their slaves with them.[35]

Another provision in regard to slaves, besides their importation, was a section on the protection of their persons:

> Any person who shall maliciously dismember or deprive a slave of life shall suffer such punishment as would be inflicted in case the like offence had been committed on a free white person, and on the like proof, except in case of insurrection by such slave, and unless such death should happen by accident in giving such slave moderate correction.[36]

[34] A term frequently violated. Coulter, *op. cit.*, p. 259.

[35] Free Negroes were not desired in the State. According to an act of 1801 no slave was to be freed, a provision which many evaded. (*Ibid*, p. 260). If a free Negro came to the State he had to register (Act 1793), but in 1818 he was prohibited from entering. In 1852 those in the State had to pay a toll of $5.00 annually. In 1859 vagrants could be sold, the burden of proof of freedom being in the Negro himself. Free Negroes were not citizens, were subject to trial in slave courts and were forbidden to carry arms, dispense medicine, set type, read, give testimony. The laws here again were not observed. (*Ibid*, pp. 260-261). The first ordained minister of color in Savannah was George Leile who was liberated by Henry Sharp, of Burke County and afterwards became pastor of a church in Kingston, Jamaica. "During his short stay in Savannah he baptized, among others, Andrew and his wife Hannah, and Hazar, belonging to the Honorable Jonathan Bryan and by whom they were made free." (White, *Collections*, p. 313). Andrew became a preacher in his master's barn. On January 20, 1788, he was "ordained by the Reverend Abraham Marshall and a colored minister named Jesse Peter from the vicinity of Augusta and constituted the first colored Baptist Church in Savannah consisting of 69 members." (*Ibid*).

[36] A number of laws followed on this section to protect the slave from injury or abuse by the owner, overseer or free white person. There was to be no unnecessary or excess whipping, and physical injury was punishable. The slave was to be properly fed and clothed, was not to be required to do excessive labor, or unnecessary work on Sunday. The master was to defend the slave, when he was accused of crime, and pay his court costs. The slave was entitled to bail at the discretion of the judge in jail cases if the white man under similar circumstances were bailable, and in non-jail cases on *certiorari* to the justice of the peace, providing the owner gave bond to not less than double the value of the slave. The owner might apply to the governor for a pardon for the slave who meanwhile was entitled to a suspension of sentence. An amendment of 1863 provided that

In the Constitution of 1798, Georgia again demonstrated an interest in the "arts and sciences," leaving it to the legislature to give further donations and privileges and provide effectual measures for improvement and security of funds.[37]

Finally, the Constitution-makers, perhaps feeling confident of the adequacy of their work, submitted the Constitution, with no provision for the calling of a new convention to make any alterations in the future. They decided that if any alteration were needed, a bill for the purpose specifying the needs would have to be read three times in each house on three separate days, requiring a two-thirds vote thereon. If the bill passed it would be published six months prior to the next annual election of the General Assembly. If, in their first meeting thereafter, two-thirds of each branch voted upon it after hearing it three separate days, then and then only should the Constitution be amended. Such amendments, as has been said, took place only twenty-three times.

---

justifiable homicide was the slave's only defense in murder cases; if he could get no one to defend him, the court must appoint one attorney, or more, who upon acquittal obtained the right to the slave as his property. (Cobb's *Digest*, Acts 1851, 1859, 1860, 1863). Penal laws for slaves divided crimes into two classes, those which entailed jail sentences and those which did not. Jail cases were capital crimes committed by slaves (the classification was not the same for whites) and consisted of attempt to poison, to commit rape on a free white female; assault on a free white person with intent to murder or with a weapon liable to cause death; maiming a free white person; burglary; arson of all kinds as contained in the Penal Code, except arson in cities and towns. (Classification and other details taken from *Georgia Bar Association Reports* 1909, pp. 232-233.) Jail cases were tried by a jury in the Superior Court and death or a proportionate sentence was administered.

All other criminal cases, non-jail, were tried by the justice of the peace. The trial began with an arrest on warrant by the justice of the peace who called two other justices to preside with him. The sentence was corporal punishment, not extending to depriving of life or member. (*Ibid*).

[37] An act of 1817 provided $250,000 for poor schools. In 1818 every tenth and one-hundredth lots in seven new counties were appropriated for the cause of education. In 1821 $250,000 was allowed for county academies. George White, *Statistics of the State of Georgia*, 1849, p. 70.

## CHAPTER VIII

## THE CONSTITUTION OF 1798 IN ACTION

### 1. How the Constitution of 1798 Functioned

That Georgia had a Constitution which functioned with little change for sixty-odd years speaks well for its stability.

During these years 1798-1861, one can assume that the Constitution was constantly referred to. The legislature, perhaps, consulted the document in the process of passing a law. So, too, must the executive have been conscious of it as he executed the laws. The last word on the constitutionality of any action, civilian, legislative, executive, is to be found in the records of cases which came before the courts.

Probably very near to the average man as he went about his daily tasks was the judiciary—the justices of the peace, the sheriffs, the ordinaries, the judges. He had a great respect for the superior court judge, who gradually acquired more and more prestige. Instead of each judge being supreme in his own district, it came about, by common consent, that judges held conventions in order to bring some of their decisions into line with others. Finally came the establishment of the Supreme Court,[1] and the steady growth in its status and power.

### II. How the Constitution was Invoked—Before the Establishment of the Supreme Court in 1845

All the revolutionary court records prior to 1779 were lost, except those of Wilkes County, but the situation there may have been typical. There was no courthouse in this county until 1785, the court being held in private houses or outdoors. The jury sometimes sat on a log while consulting on what the verdict should be.[2] A far cry was this rough-and-ready justice

---

[1] By this time the judges had assumed two functions: (a) to judge cases on the merit of their constitutionality; (b) to interpret for the legislature the constitutionality of its acts.

[2] Smith, *op. cit.*, p. 137.

of the revolutionary era from the elaborate judicial system which was brought over on the *Anne*.[3] Indictments were made for profane swearing, fighting and gambling, Sabbath-breaking, playing fives, failure of the militia officers to patrol at night. The constitutional ground on which the indictments rested is not stated, but one may assume it was local police power.

The first record found of early decisions was that covering the years 1805-1810.[4] In that day the judges put their decisions in writing only when the case was appealed. " Decisions of the first importance are left to float upon the memories of

---

[3] The first jury functioned in 1773 in Savannah, when

> to this bench of magistrates the trustees did what they could to give dignity and authority, and well knowing the respect which is inspired by the badges and trappings of office, sent over magisterial gowns; those for the three bailiffs being purple, edged with fur and for the Recorder being black tufted. (White, *Statistics*, p. 59).
>
> The trustees purchased a " copper-gilt mace " costing the equivalent of $500.00 and a seal costing $150.00 " or perhaps five times the value of the log house in which the court was held. Without all the trappings, however, the lawyers licensed under the first Constitution were still recognizable, for it was the habit to carry a green bag and they should be heard in the " Habit of a Black Robe." (*Georgia Bar Association Reports*, 1913, pp. 52-96.)

There persisted in Georgia much English practice, the common law, the *habeas corpus*, written charges to grand jury, the use of laymen as assistants in courts, trover for recovery of slaves, " ravishment of ward " (adopted by guardians seeking to regain possession of kidnapped wards), warrant for Hue and Cry to arrest the captor of stolen slaves, assize of bread, banishment, admiralty cases, benefit of clergy (not abolished until 1817), branding with M for manslaughter, F for forgery, T for theft. In the governor's commission he was provided with a general court which seems to be the original of the Superior Court adopted in 1777, with the powers of King's Bench, Common Pleas and Exchequer and with a separate court of Chancery to be held before governor and council for equity. Scanty records indicate the type of suit in those days—Civil suits on bonds, accounts, trespass, sedition, imprisonment for debt, ecclesiastical offenses, and an active business in criminal suits. Usually conviction was sure and the penalty heavy, from pillory, stocks, whipping, to hanging by the neck until dead. (*Ibid*, pp. 77-96).

[4] T. U. P. Charlton, *Reports of Cases Argued and Determined in the Superior Courts of the Eastern Circuit of Georgia, 1805-1810*. This was financed by Stephen Gould of New York and published in 1824.

the gentlemen of the Bar."[5] A rich body of decisions and precedents has no doubt been lost. About 1821, it became the custom to put all decisions in the minutes. Most of the records from 1805 to 1810 are of routine points or technical questions of procedure. Few details are given of the cases, no argument of counsel appears, and only occasionally is there a statement as to who were the lawyers and the attorney of the State.

The judges were called upon to determine all appeals from the inferior court, sit in judgment on appeals from the court of ordinary, determine all equity cases, expound the law of divorce, " to be in fact, the last hope of not only the criminal but also the lawyer, for there was no tribunal to correct his error."[6]

The circuit riding judge of those days

> was a splendid figure in the epic era of our Commonwealth, when unfettered by a Code, unenlightened and unbefogged by a maze of discussions through which to search for the last one on the point at issue, he drew for judgment on the rich treasury of the common law, and listened to the rare eloquence of a royal race of advocates, who came to the forum fresh from communion with nature in her wild, uncultured beauty . . . Their conventions at which points of practice were discussed and decisions on important topics read and approved or rejected by a majority vote have been preserved in the volumes of Dudley and Charlton . . . gems of legal lore.[7]

The Constitution, as amended in 1835, had called for a Supreme Court for the correction of errors; but the legislature had disregarded the provision entirely. Each judge in his own circuit was independent of all others, therefore the same law was often differently construed in different circuits. The Judiciary Act of 1799 had called for annual meetings of the judges at the seat of government, but no such meetings were

---

[5] Charlton, *op. cit.*, Introduction.

[6] R. M. Charlton, *Reports of Decisions made in the Superior Court of the Eastern District of Georgia, 1811-1837*, Introduction.

[7] *Georgia Bar Association Reports* (1887), p. 94.

held, and the Act was repealed in 1801. Only at their infrequent conventions were the judges able to compare and confer.

The conventions were legalized in 1830, but not before the judges had been reprimanded for holding them. At one of their conventions held at Augusta, the judges—J. M. Berrien, R. Walker, Y. Gresham and S. Harris—declared unanimously that the Alleviating Acts, which were preventing the collection of debts and almost closing the courts to all civil suits, were unconstitutional. The legislature promptly reprimanded the judges:

> The extraordinary power of determining upon the Constitutionality of acts of the State Legislature, if yielded by the General Assembly whilst it is not given by the constitution of laws of the state, would be an abandonment of the dearest rights and liberties of the people which we, their representatives, are bound to guard and protect inviolate.[8]

The Conventions were legalized and the brightest names in Georgia's legal history may be found in these records:[9] William H. Crawford (Judge, Senator, Cabinet Member, Presidential nominee), L. Q. C. Lamar (who served from Mississippi in the Cabinet, Senate and Supreme Court), Hiram Warner (later Chief Justice of Georgia's Supreme Court). These men bemoaned the need of a Supreme Court since their decisions were merely advisory and not enforceable.

It is fascinating to try to picture the meeting of the Superior Court on the two great occasions of the year, when Judge T. U. P. Charlton, follower of the Troup-Crawford-Jackson Party, might preside, or the renowned Judge Wayne.[10] The people gathered from miles around, probably bringing whatever crops the season produced (the court met in different

---

[8] C. C. Haines, *The American Doctrine of Judicial Supremacy*, p. 260.

[9] G. M. Dudley, *Reports of the Decisions Made by the Judges of Superior Courts of Law and Chancery of the State of Georgia (1821-1833)*.

[10] Princeton graduate, legislator, Mayor of Savannah, State and Federal Judge, later Justice of the Federal Supreme Court.

THE CONSTITUTION OF 1798 IN ACTION      95

months in different places, the legislature having worked out a schedule of meetings). There was the hum and bustle of the big town of Savannah or Augusta, cosmopolitan in their contacts because they were commercial centers; the excitement in the little town of Louisville, one of whose claims to distinction is that it once served as the capital of the State; the crowding of wagons and teams around the public square of Milledgeville, another future capital.

One may picture, on court days,[11] gatherings around some such lawyer as Robert Augustus Beall, holding forth on the report of the Committee of Twenty-one, in 1832, which protested usurpation of powers by the Federal government, or Augustin S. Clayton, who, in 1830, declared that

> without intending the least disrespect to that court to whose constitutional authority this and all other State courts will, I hope, cheerfully submit, this question (The Butler and Worcester case) can never go up from a court in which I preside until the people of the State yield it.[12]

Or one might see Peter Early telling the crowd how he served on the committee of the House which impeached Justice Chase.

An act of 1841 required judges of the Superior Courts to write out their decisions for the governor, who must publish them.[13]

The few records prior to the establishment of the Supreme Court in 1845, evince a type of case similar to that of any other period. Some of the issues involved *habeas corpus* [14] and *ex post facto*.[15] Removal of the disabilities of the Confiscation

---

[11] See Stephen F. Miller, *Bench and Bar of Georgia*, for thirty-three sketches of the high points in Georgia's legal history.

[12] *Ibid*, sketch of Clayton.

[13] J. M. McCafferty, *Decisions of the Superior Courts of the State of Georgia* (1842-1843).

[14] Charlton, *Reports of Cases*, State v. De Las Maurignos, May 1805 (p. 24), State v. Patterson, August, 1810 (p. 311), State v. Plime, December 1807 (p. 142), State v. Wederstrandt, June 1808 (p. 213).

[15] White v. Wayne, *Ibid*, (pp. 94-108).

96  A CONSTITUTIONAL HISTORY OF GEORGIA

Act of 1782 [16] was another issue. There was a controversy as to whether alleviation of debts by deferment of payment was or was not an infringement of the obligation of contracts.[17] Any measure which would lessen the value of contracts would be violation of contract, but the judge considered alleviation a mere deferment.

To Judge Berrien's [18] court came a challenge of an ordinance of the City of Savannah,[19] imposing a tax on all goods not produced in the State, sold on commission by any person residing in the city. It was held that such a tax was not an impost or duty on imports but the legitimate exercise of the State's power to regulate its internal commerce. The decision in another case [20] exempted from levy and sale " two beds and bedding, common bedsteads, a spining wheel and two pair of cards, a loom, cow and calf, common tools of his trade and cooking utensils and ten dollars worth of provisions," plus the family Bible; thus showing a desire on the part of the courts to protect the interests of debtors.

Other proceedings recorded were concerned with jurisdiction,[21] a liquor inspection law which had been evaded, bringing a penalty of $30.00,[22] and a woman's will.[23] The decision in the latter case was that,

16 Johnston *v.* White, *Ibid,* (p. 141).

17 Grimwald *v.* Ross, *Ibid,* (p. 175).

18 It was of Judge Berrien that Chief Justice Marshall spoke when he referred to the " honey-tongued Georgia youth ". Many thought the mantle of Chief Justice would fall upon his shoulders. He refused a position later on the Georgia Supreme Court bench on the grounds that he could not decide legal questions while travelling around without books, and without the time to ponder upon them. (Sketch by S. F. Miller, *Bench and Bar of Georgia,* I).

19 Charlton, *Reports of Decisions,* p. 26.

20 *Ibid,* p. 108.

21 Charlton, *Reports of Decisions,* p. 316, John Low *v.* Commissioners of Pilotage (Jan. 1830).

22 *Ibid,* p. 368.

23 *Ibid,* p. 184.

## THE CONSTITUTION OF 1798 IN ACTION 97

it seems that the will of a *femme couvert* will have no efficacy, unless there be an agreement before marriage giving her the power to make such will, or such right has been conferred on her after marriage, by some act analogous to an agreement before marriage—the mere parole assent of her husband is not sufficient to give such a will validity.

As one imagines the scenes on court days, one is reminded of the fact that slaves were present, perhaps as personal servants or farm hands, and that on these occasions there would probably be public auctions. There would also be test cases in the courts regarding slaves and free persons of color, and the right to manumit one's slaves by will.[24]

Two *habeas corpus* cases throw light on the rights of free persons of color:

> All of every condition, of every country and of every complexion, are equally entitled to it, the native of South Africa, not less than the Peer of the Realm.[25]

Distinction was made between the denial to a slave of *habeas corpus* and the protection of his life and members by the Constitution:[26]

> They have secured to them formal trial for all offenses, and the right of examining witnesses and in capital cases the right of trial by jury. They cannot be tried twice for the same offense . . . Their persons are protected from violence and cruelty, none but the Master having the right causelessly to strike or whip them and the Master himself being restrained

---

24 The manumission of slaves was punishable by the Act of 1801 and the penalties increased by the Act of 1818, so that the will of a man in behalf of his servants, Amy and Thomas, was voided. (R. M. Charlton, *Reports of Decisions*, pp. 178-179).

One could take one's slaves out of the State and free them without penalty. The General Assembly in 1827 protested an appropriation of money by Congress for the American Colonization Society. (Catterall, *Judicial Cases Concerning Slavery*, p. 1, and Charlton, *Reports of Decisions*, p. 542).

25 Dudley, *op. cit.*, pp. 42, 46.

26 Dudley, *op. cit.*, pp. 51-52.

to such moderate chastisement as may be necessary for discipline and the preservation of a just subordination. . . . Secured . . . all care, food, sustenance and clothing . . . and an exemption from excessive labor.

In summarizing these early records, it would appear that the judges grew in importance. The right to pass upon the constitutionality of legislation was assumed but not overworked and there appeared to be close cooperation between the legislative and judicial branches of the government.

### III. THE CONSTITUTION AND THE SUPREME COURT —AFTER 1845

The legislature passed an amendment to the Constitution in 1835 [27] which ten years later was put into operation as Article III, Section 1 of the Constitution. This act created for Georgia [28] a Supreme Court of three judges,[29] elected by the legislature to serve six years. It was to be a court for the correction of error. Arrangements were made for the service of a reporter and the regular publication of the proceedings of the court.[30] Fear of delay led to the insertion of the clause that cases must be disposed of at the first term. The first panel of judges consisted of the Whigs, Joseph Lumpkin [31] and E. A.

[27] Requirement for amendment then was a two-thirds vote of each house for two consecutive years.

[28] In the *Georgia Bar Association Reports,* 1907, J. R. Lamar gives the *History of the Establishment of the Supreme Court of Georgia.*

[29] From the beginning, one of the three judges was chosen to serve as Chief Justice. Such positions were held by Joseph H. Lumpkin from 1845-1867; H. Warner 1867, 1872-1880; Joseph E. Brown, 1868-1870; Osborne A. Lochrane 1870-1872; James Jackson 1880-1887; Logan E. Bleckley 1887-1895; T. J. Simmons, 1895-1905; W. H. Fish, 1905-1923; R. B. Russell, 1923-1941; Charles S. Reid, 1941-1943; R. C. Bell, 1943-1945.

[30] *Reports of Cases Decided in the Supreme Court of the State of Georgia,* Introduction, *Georgia Reports,* Volume 1.

[31] Lumpkin served as Chief Justice from 1845-1867. He had the task of establishing the prestige of the court and making uniform the administration of the law. A master workman, he avoided technicalities, and proceeded to the innate merit of the case.

Nisbet,[32] and the Democrat, Hiram Warner.[33] It has been said of this triumvirate that they were like three great columns, one Corinthian, one Gothic, and one Doric;[34] that Lumpkin was given to "rich and captivating eloquence," Nisbet to a "smooth classic style," and Warner to "clear, lucid line and the logic of argument." [35]

The records of the Supreme Court [36] show the mounting confidence of the people in a court of last resort. Early hostility to judicial revision disappeared and it came to be accepted as a boon.[37]

Among the cases appealed to the new Supreme Court were some involving personal rights, such as the right to bear arms and to have a fair trial. Others were concerned with land lotteries, with eminent domain, with rights of newly created businesses, taxation, school funds, and, approaching 1860, with the status of Negroes, whether slave or free. Through the story, like two threads of a pattern, are the questions of delegation of power and police power.

[32] Nisbet was of the Jeffersonian States' Rights school, but opposed nullification, supported Clay in 1844, the Compromise of 1850, the American Party in 1856. He proposed the unanimity of signature to the Ordinance of Secession.

[33] Warner was a farmer-judge. He served on the court from 1845-1853, and in Congress, 1855-1857. In 1860 he was a member of the secession convention opposing secession but signed the document. Appointed Chief Justice in 1867, he was reduced to Associate by the reconstruction government. He served as Chief Justice from 1872 until his resignation in 1880. During the more than thirty-four years that he served in the Court, Warner took part in 1,969 decisions, of which 78 were dissenting. (68 *Georgia* 847.)

[34] *Ibid*, p. 855.

[35] *Ibid*, p. 852.

[36] Index-Digests of these volumes have been published from time to time, Volumes 1-100 by Howard Van Epps and John W. Akin (3 vs.) 1899; 101-148 by George W. Stevens and Bascom S. Deaver (4 vs.) 1921; 149-162 by L. T. Gillen (2 vs.) 1927; 163-179 by Dale F. Stansbury (2 vs.) 1935. The Digest of Volumes 180-198 was not available for this monograph.

[37] In 1906 a Court of Appeals was established to relieve the pressure on the Supreme Court.

100  A CONSTITUTIONAL HISTORY OF GEORGIA

The purpose of an examination of cases prior to the Civil War is to note shifting interests and to determine the working relationship between the branches of government. If change should develop it is likely it would appear in the decisions.

Infringement of personal rights was no new subject in the courts. Carrying a pistol, in violation of " an act to guard and protect the citizens of this State against the unwarrantable and too prevalent use of deadly weapons," was the charge in one of the cases.[38] According to the act:

> Bowie or other knives (to be worn) as arms of offense or defense, pistols, dirks, swords-canes, spears, etc., shall be contemplated in this act, save such pistols as are known and used as horsemen's pistols.[39]

One might carry weapons only if one carried them openly. The judge disposed of the question thus:

> The Constitution, in declaring that every citizen has the right to bear arms in defense of himself and the State, has neither expressly nor by implication denied to the legislature the right to enact laws in regard to the manner in which arms shall be borne. . . .[40] A law which merely inhibits the wearing of certain weapons in a concealed manner is valid. But so far as it cuts off the exercise of the right of the citizen altogether to bear arms, or under the color of prescribing the mode, renders the right itself, useless, it is in conflict with the Federal and State Constitutions and void. . . . Our opinion is that any law, State or Federal, is repugnant to the Constitution and void which contravenes this right originally belonging to our forefathers, trampled under foot by Charles I and his two wicked sons and successors, re-established by the Revolution of 1688, conveyed to this land of liberty by the colonists, and finally incorporated conspicuously in our own Magna Charta. And Lexington, Concord, Camden, River

38 1 *Ga.* 243 (1846). The act challenged was that of December 25, 1837.
39 *Ibid*, p. 246.
40 *Ibid*, p. 249.

Raisin, Sandusky, and the laurel-crowned field of New Orleans plead eloquently for this interpretation! And the acquisition of Texas may be considered the full fruits of this great constitutional right.[41]

The legislature was vindicated, and a little political propaganda in regard to Texas was thrown in for good measure.

Appeals were taken also in other cases involving denial of personal rights, particularly the right of fair trial.[42] When a jury was challenged, a system of " triors " was used, two indifferent men named by the court selecting two jurors, these two getting three others.[43]

The courts were called upon to settle ownership of disputed land. When terms of a lottery act were not met, land was regranted by Act. This brought litigation to determine the constitutionality of the Act.[44]

That the Georgia judges were well posted on great legal opinions is evidenced not only by frequent references to Story, Kent, and Blackstone but also by calling attention to important decisions in other states and in the Federal Supreme Court. In these days when Georgia was growing with the rest of the nation, identical situations arose in various places; especially was this the case in questions about waterways, bridges, tolls, and railroads.[45]

41 1 *Ga.* 325, 251.

42 1 *Ga.* 616. An Act of 1843 changed the Penal Code to allow the State to call separate prisoners as witnesses against others, to stop the practice then prevailing of including all persons who were present at an offense in order to exclude their testimony.

43 1 *Ga.* 619.

44 2 *Ga.* 143 (1847) Lotteries were common. This particular one specified that persons should be appointed to take names, at twenty-five cents per name, before the drawing. At the drawing, if one were lucky, he would receive a tract of land in fee simple, on the payment of eighteen dollars within two years time or forfeit.

45 3 *Ga.* 31 (1847) Irvinton Bridge Company case. Eminent Domain and property rights were recognized in proper spheres but a "higher law" was also appealed to. 3 *Ga.* 333 (1847) Macon and Western Railroad case

102   A CONSTITUTIONAL HISTORY OF GEORGIA

Attempted delegations of power belonging to the courts were frustrated. An Act of December 1837,

> to authorize the governor, secretary of state, surveyor-general and comptroller general, to correct any error that may have taken place in issuing any grant or grants in any of the land lotteries of this state, passed December 22, 1827

was a case in point.[46] The judge found that the interpretation of justice was a power properly attached to the judiciary department.[47] " The Court is thus divested of its appropriate and indeed exclusive function—the trial of the right of property in lands ";[48] if the government recalled grants to one thing, it can to all causes; " if it can at all, it is a pure despotism." Since the Act of 1837 provided no jury trial and " no man can be divested of his property but by the judgment of his peers ", the Court consigned the governor to his own sphere of activity.

Another suit charging unconstitutionality on the basis of delegation of power [49] involved an Act of 1843 prescribing the method of incorporating companies for certain purposes:

> When persons interested shall desire to have any church, campground, manufacturing company, trading company, bridge company, ferry company, incorporated, they shall petition in writing the Superior or Inferior Court of the county . . . (giving object, privilege, name and style,) . . . and said court shall pass a rule or order directing said petition to be entered of record on the minutes of said court.[50]

---

(" Our State is perhaps second to none in the union in its magnificent system of railroads " said Judge Lumpkin, p. 338). Again private rights were respected but an appeal was made on behalf of transportation development. 5 *Ga.* 194-217 (1848) Flint River Steamboat case. An appeal for fair trial by jury against a suit for payment of wages.

46 7 *Ga.* 172 (1849).
47 *Ibid*, p. 176.
48 Prince, *Digest*, 909, 910.
49 14 *Ga.* 80 (1853).
50 14 *Ga.* 81.

## THE CONSTITUTION OF 1798 IN ACTION 103

The judge who originally heard the case declared the act unconstitutional. On appeal, the lower court was reversed, since the act clothed the courts with no new powers or discretion, but with ministerial acts. "With the policy of these Statutes, we have nothing to do. The province of this and all other courts is "*jus dicere* not *jus dare*." [51]

Sometimes the right of local taxation and the exercise of police power was challenged. In the case of the Mayor of Macon *v.* Macon and Western Railroad Company,[52] the right of the city (by the Act of 1847), to regulate tolls on the bridge over the Ocmulgee River, thus repealing other acts, was questioned.[53] The railroad had been granted a monopoly over its route, but nothing was said about the haul by dray through the city and across the bridge. The tolls "the city had fixed according to the ordinance of 1849 were necessary to keep the bridge in good order." The right of the company to use the bridge without compensation was declared not apparent.

One of the most important of the early charges of unconstitutionality, on this occasion on the basis of the United States Constitution, was the case of Padelford, Fay and Company versus the Mayor of Savannah.[54] An ordinance of the city of Savannah announced that after January 1842, fifty cents on every hundred dollars should be paid on the gross sales of Negroes, and wares of any kind. Padelford, Fay and Company refused to pay the tax on goods imported into the State and sold by them in the original cases and packages. The grounds they cited were: (1) only Congress has the power to regulate commerce, and (2) no State may lay imposts and duties except as necessary for inspection laws. The opinion of the court is one

---

51 *Ibid*, p. 86.

52 7 *Ga.* 221.

53 The original provision had been that for the sum of $25,000 the city acquired the bridge from the State. The corporation was forbidden to charge toll on any wagon or carriage loaded with cotton or corn.

54 14 *Ga.* 438 (January 1854). Overruled 84 *Ga.* 759 (1890).

of the longest of the early decisions.[55] The adopting conventions of six of the original thirteen states were analyzed to show the reaction of the early statesmen against interference by the United States with taxation.[56] The State is supreme, the judge declared, on reserved powers, the United States on delegated powers and on concurrent powers both are supreme. The ordinance in question, being of a concurrent nature and having been in effect twelve years without a protest from Congress, was held valid on the grounds of police power.[57]

In 1857, came the first cases in which the judges' dissenting opinions were given.[58]

The rights of free Negroes came up, at times, for clearance. An Act of 1818[59] had denied the right of purchase or acquisition of lands to "free persons of color." This Act was repealed by an Act of 1819,[60] (except for the cities of Savannah, Augusta, and Darien). Judge Lumpkin grudgingly admitted the constitutionality of the act:[61]

> While therefore I exceedingly doubt the policy of allowing free negroes to acquire and hold real estate and that, too, with-

[55] "It was said afterwards that Judge Benning's opinion in the case was largely a reproduction of his speech in the State Rights Convention at Memphis over which Judge McDonald presided. The war killed that decision as it did the Dred Scott case decision and both are buried in the same grave." *Georgia Bar Association Reports*, 1909, p. 134.

[56] He reviewed the experiences from the Chisholm case (2 Dallas 419) on, which tended to prove that Georgia was a believer in strict construction of the Constitution regardless of political party preference. The resolutions in the test cases of Worcester and Butler *v.* Georgia (6 Peters 515) and Tassels and Graves *v.* Georgia (5 Peters 1) were signed by two separate political parties.

[57] One interesting sidelight and reflection strikes a modern slant when the judge remarked that anyway it is the consumer who always pays.

[58] 23 *Ga.* 82 (1857).

[59] Cobb's *Digest of Laws of the State of Georgia Prior to 1851*, p. 943.

[60] *Ibid*, p. 995.

[61] 25 *Ga.* 441 (1858).

# THE CONSTITUTION OF 1798 IN ACTION

out limitations as to quantity, still the correction of the evil if it be one, is with the Legislature and not with the Courts.

Another comment of Judge Lumpkin's merits notice:

> Notwithstanding the judiciary is the weakest of the three departments of government and is therefore less dangerous to public liberty than either of the other two, still it is both the right and duty of all courts to declare all acts void which plainly and palpably violate the Constitution.

The early Conventions made no attempt at social legislation or protection of morals. It would seem that the State had not awakened to a keen sense of social responsibility. Earlier laws on such subjects as gaming were re-passed in the Adopting Act of 1784,[62] and the attitude toward them may be found in the remarks:

> There have been giants in Georgia both at the bar and in the counsels of state and it behooves us if we would be respected by our posterity to manifest a becoming reverence for the teachings of our fathers.[63]

Though the judges were always careful to accede that the legislature represents the will of the people, the sovereigns in Georgia, nevertheless they permitted no interference with or regulation of the techniques of procedure of the courts.[64]

The right of the Superior Court to decide upon the constitutionality of acts of the legislature was asserted,[65] but unless there were obvious and strong reasons to declare to the contrary, the presumption was always that the act was constitutional.[66]

Since the formation of the court, the greater number of cases seems to test rights of trial, contract, and delegation of

---

[62] 28 *Ga.* 339 (1859).
[63] *Ibid*, p. 338.
[64] Bond *et. al. v.* Munroe, *e. g.* 28 *Ga.* 597.
[65] 10 *Ga.* 190.
[66] 8 *Ga.* 312, 9 *Ga.* 253, etc.

power.[67] There is no special theme. On the whole, one gathers that each case is an entity; that justice to the best of the court's opinion is to be dealt, and that the best way to obtain that justice is by the cooperation of legislature and judiciary. The assumption seems to be that the legislators have acted in good faith. In several cases, the judges urge some constraint upon the contestants to abide by some common higher law.

Georgia people settled their problems in the home courts. The Federal Courts had long been established in Georgia but they were " almost unknown to the people of the interior until after the war, and outside Savannah, Augusta, and Brunswick, not one lawyer in one hundred attempted to practice in a United States Court." [68] Appeal was seldom made to the Federal Supreme Court.

By amendment, the Constitution, during the years from 1798 to 1861, reduced the power of the legislature, abolished property qualifications and enlarged the number of elective offices. In so much it was responsive to the needs of the time. From the above samples of its testing in the courts, it would appear that the enlargement of the scope of the judiciary was satisfactory to the people. Popular election of the executive brought some confusion. In allocation of powers, challenged as delegation, it was difficult to maintain a complete separation of power into three departments. Judicial review was practised. Added to this right, the Supreme Court was increasingly burdened with contests involving personal rights and property rights.

How much the Constitution of 1798 would have failed to meet the needs of the State after 1860 there is no way of knowing, since the war years and reconstruction brought other Constitutions.

[67] One might also list cases tested on the ground of an act containing matter different from that defined in the title 4 *Ga.* 26 (1848), 12 *Ga.* 36 (1852) and 6 *Ga.* 151 (1849); and a case in regard to injury to livestock by railroads, 17 *Ga.* 323 (1855).

[68] *Georgia Bar Association Reports,* 1909, p. 135.

# CHAPTER IX
## GEORGIA FROM 1798 TO 1861

THE period during which Georgia lived under its third Constitution, 1798-1861, was one of steady growth. The State reflected the changes that were taking place in the nation. Primarily a Jeffersonian section, Georgia reversed the usual classification of followers of the national parties. The Federalists were found among the democratic frontiersmen, whereas the Jeffersonians were the aristocratic tidewater element led by James Jackson, W. H. Crawford, George Troup, and T. U. P. Charlton.[1] As the Federalists became weaker and weaker, Georgia split into factions, voting for personalities rather than principles.[2] The plan of having the legislature elect the governor[3] was conducive to factionalism, lobbying, and heated campaigns. A national issue was needed. The tariff issue and the nullification issue finally centered men's thoughts on measures rather than men, and the local Troup-Clarke fights were forgotten.

Being, in the main, Democratic-Republican, Georgia cast its electoral vote for Jefferson, Madison, and Monroe. Monroe visited the State in 1819. Hospitality was lavished on him as it had been on Washington. He took a trip on the "City of Savannah" before it sailed on its famous voyage. In the campaign of 1824 the vote went to a favorite son, W. H. Crawford. At the same time that John Quincy Adams won the presidential election, the States' Rights partisans secured the governorship for George M. Troup, a Crawford follower. The amicable federal relations were threatened. A contest immediately arose with the United States over administration of Indian lands and treaties with the tribes of Cherokees and

---

[1] Coulter, *op. cit.*, pp. 223-226.

[2] Hezekiah Niles wrote "we know not what they differ about—but they do violently differ." Cited in Coulter, *op. cit.*, p. 226.

[3] Changed in 1824 to popular election.

Creeks. Georgia, in the first half of the nineteenth century, did not seriously consider severing the union. Being jealous of its prestige and of those rights which it believed were reserved, it quarreled with President Adams, issued a protest against the tariff of 1828, and defied Chief Justice Marshall. But it rejected threats to the union. It took time from local and national quarrels to welcome Lafayette in 1825. Marshals of the day (Sunday, March 27) "met on the East bank of the Oconee the procession accompanying General Lafayette" to conduct him into Milledgeville, the capital. A ball and supper were given for him at the State House in Milledgeville and a barbecue was served on the grounds. [4]

Jeffersonian agrarian for the first two decades of the century, Georgia turned to Jackson in the elections of 1828 and 1832. In the course of his two terms came the culmination of an internal conflict which found expression in both local and national affairs at this time. The old contest between lower and upper Georgia, between the settled community and the frontier, flared up. Standard bearer for the old James Jackson—W. H. Crawford alliance of lower Georgia was Governor Troup, while John Clarke led the up-country faction. Every election was hotly contested by Troupites and Clarkites with every method of publicity known to political campaigns of the day, duels, cards, competitions in verse and prose. Tax lists were compared and mass meetings were held. [5] By the time of Jackson's Force Bill the Troupites had become the local States' Rights party, while the Clarkites had become Democrats.[6]

In 1832 the South Carolina move for nullification of the Tariff Act was rejected,—not, however, without a struggle. Public meetings were held throughout Georgia and the people passed resolutions that they "would dress in their own home-

---

[4] Leola S. Beeson, *History Stories of Milledgeville and Baldwin County*, pp. 36 and 40.

[5] T. Gamble, *Savannah Duels and Duellists*, 1733-1877, pp. 115, 116, 229.

[6] Union men or Unionists.

spun instead of Yankee cloth, that they would eat their own hogs instead of meat raised in Kentucky and that they would walk rather than ride on Western ponies." [7] The women took part in the protest, and "wives urged their husbands in Congress to appear at the sessions . . . in homespun suits." The anti-Tariff Convention in Milledgeville in 1832 witnessed a classic debate between Berrien and Forsyth which lasted three days. [8] Though nullification was favored by many outstanding men such as W. H. Crawford and J. M. Berrien, even these leaders did not intend that such defiance should entail eventual disunion; and indeed there were prominent leaders—for example John Forsyth and Wilson Lumpkin—who were altogether opposed to the policy. In 1833, at a meeting of States' Rights advocates, a committee of thirteen [9] drew up resolutions.

The year 1833 saw, too, a convention for reducing representation in the General Assembly and readjusting the basis of apportionment. The recommendations were rejected by the voters at the next election. A similar effort to change representation failed in a convention in 1839.

By 1840 the States' Rights party, under the leadership of John M. Berrien, A. H. Stephens and Robert Toombs, had taken the name of Whig. In that year Georgia voted for the Whig candidate, W. H. Harrison. In 1844 it voted for the Democrats and Polk, but in 1848 it again went Whig and voted for Taylor. The Whigs were the dominant party in the State from 1834 to 1854. There were two periods in their history, the first when they allied themselves with the National Party and approved compromise measures to hold the union together; the second when the slavery issue became more and more dominant. The Southern Whigs resorted to the title of "Cotton Whigs", as opposed to "Conscience Whigs." Many

---

7 Beeson, *op. cit.*, p. 44.

8 *Ibid*, p. 45.

9 They consisted in part of A. S. Clayton, Crawford and Augustus Beall.

under the leadership of Robert Toombs and A. H. Stephens, formed a Constitutional Union Party and eventually drifted back into the Democratic fold. Many went into a Southern Rights Party. Some, such as Benjamin H. Hill, E. A. Nisbet and John M. Berrien, became for a time Know-Nothings. The Democrats were in control of Georgia by 1849. Pierce and Buchanan won Georgia's vote in 1852 and 1856.

The public figures of Georgia, in their efforts to find a party congenial to them, differed as did statesmen of other states on the tariff, on banking, and on internal improvement. But upon one point they agreed. This was the subject of the right of Congress to prohibit slavery in the territories. In 1850 Georgia had participated in the Nashville Convention on the subject of the Compromise Bill. In 1850 it also held its own convention at Milledgeville, [10] out of which came the Georgia Platform which helped defer the conflict for another ten years. Charles J. Jenkins, who was to figure in so much of Georgia's constitutional history, was chairman of the committee of thirty-three which made the report on December thirteenth representing the victory of the union over disunion. In no uncertain terms, however, was included the statement that Georgia would not tolerate any interference with the rights of a territory to apply for statehood because of the existence of slavery there. Feeling that this positive statement by a pivotal state of the South would prevent any future trouble, and that the prompt execution of the Fugitive Slave Law would obviate any further difficulties on this score, Georgia prepared for a "business man's peace" as did the rest of the nation. In this convention Georgia resolved to raise a sum of money to purchase, for the Washington National Monument, a block of marble to bear the coat-of-arms of Georgia and the inscription "Georgia Convention, December, 1850."

The expectation of peace, however, was short-lived. The Kansas-Nebraska Bill, the organization of the Republican

---

[10] *Journal of the State Convention at Milledgeville, Tuesday, December 10, 1850.*

Party, the Lincoln-Douglas debates, John Brown's raid,—all these made for strained relations. In the election of 1860, the Democrats split. The Georgia vote was: Breckinridge, 51,893; Douglas, 11,580; and Bell, 42,855. The voters, confused, looked to the leaders for advice.[11]

In these years from 1798-1861 Georgia shared in the developments of the country—for example, in matters of banking, insurance, and shipping. Manufacturing was slow to develop in the earlier decades of the period, but the sale of cotton was generally booming, while tobacco and rice were losing to cotton. Exports increased. Georgia experienced, with the whole country, a business inflation. Some large planters moved Westward and small farmers settled in the upper counties. Lotteries were held for drawing of land in 1803, 1806, 1819, 1821, 1827, 1832, and land was remarkably easy to get.[12]

As this Westward and North-Westward movement progressed, there came a demand for better roads. There were only dirt roads until the era of the turnpike. Then private individuals chartered companies of stage coaches, or made money by establishing ferry services and toll bridges. Pressure was exerted to dredge and widen rivers and maintain militia service for protection. With the coming of steam navigation, Georgia started granting monopolies. The Gibbons v. Ogden decision (1824) put a stop to this.[13] Railroad building was encouraged, the first road being the Athens-Augusta route in 1831. The State-owned Western and Atlantic was started in 1835 and finished in 1851. Atlanta, the future capital, was built as a terminal point in 1845.

On the frontier life was primitive. People went to town only on court days. They enjoyed fist fights, horse racing, religion, and, most of all, politics. Their political philosophy was dem-

---

11 P. S. Flippin, *Herschel v. Johnson, State Rights Unionist*, p. 94.

12 See Records of Wilkes County for terms of acts and names of drawers of lots.

13 9 Wheat. 1.

ocratic. In his stories Judge Augustus B. Longstreet, the main literary figure of Georgia in this period, drew realistic pictures of the crude but kindly frontier people. Among these people the germs of what was to become independency were already present. Joseph E. Brown, who ran for governor in 1857, spoke for this section of the State when he declared that the Democratic party was the only salvation for the Union.

When Lincoln was elected, in 1860, Georgia, torn three ways as the vote showed, had to decide if it would follow South Carolina out of the Union. The legislature passed an Act in November, 1860, calling for a vote to see whether a convention should be held and for the election of delegates if the convention were authorized. The campaign was one of the most exciting in Georgia's history. The torchlight processions, barbecues, and fiery speeches in the hustings were part and parcel of the political folkways of the day. Letters bombarded the statesmen. Handbills and cards increased the printers' incomes.

The leaders divided in their opinion on secession. Robert Toombs and Alexander Stephens, bosom friends since their young manhood and hitherto agreed on every subject, differed on this one. Stephens' interests lay in the fine points of constitutional law; those of Toombs lay in commerce and industry, finance and political economy. He was considered by Stephens to be the Southern Webster.[14] Toombs' speech in the Senate, before his departure, summarized his stand. He hoped the union might be preserved through the restoration to the South of its constitutional rights—this failing, he hoped the South might depart in peace, but he was prepared for war. Howell Cobb joined Toombs, as did Governor Brown, Judge E. A. Nisbet and T. R. R. Cobb. Alexander Stephens and his dearly loved brother, Linton, joined Herschel V. Johnson in his effort to prevent the break. The State was canvassed; county mass meetings were held; "the house rocked to and fro with frenzied

---

[14] John C. Reed, *The Brothers' War*, pp. 243, 276.

applause"[15] while listening to the speeches of Toombs and Stephens; at dinner parties men "sat over their wine until a late hour."[16] When time came to vote on the convention, opinion was by no means unanimous, 50,243 voting for it and 30,123 against.[17]

15 *Ibid*, p. 267.
16 *Ibid*, p. 367.
17 Cited from P. S. Flippen, *op. cit.*, p. 172.

## CHAPTER X

## THE CONVENTION OF 1861 — SECESSION AND CONSTITUTION

The Convention which had been called by the governor on November 21, 1860, opened on January 16, 1861 in the famous old State House on the hill west of Capitol Bridge.

Every Georgian of political prominence had been elected with the exception of Governor Joseph E. Brown, Howell Cobb and Charles J. Jenkins. These were immediately asked by the Convention to take seats. The roll-call was a familiar roster including A. H. Colquitt, E. A. Nisbet, T. R. R. Cobb, Linton Stephens, H. V. Johnson, Hiram Warner, George W. Crawford, Alexander H. Stephens, Benjamin H. Hill and Robert Toombs. These statesmen were men of various political views and they differed widely on secession, but the majority favored it. Some came uninstructed.[1]

The times were exciting. South Carolina, Florida, Alabama and Mississippi had already left the Union. Emotions were tense and demonstrations were to be expected. One has a feeling of the importance of the occasion.[2] Ex-governor George W. Crawford was elected president of the Convention. He appointed a rules committee. Members were not to talk to each other during a speech; there was to be no applause or noisy demonstration; personalities were to be avoided.

At two o'clock in the afternoon of January 19 came the fateful moment. Judge E. A. Nisbet brought up a resolution for secession. Immediately, a counter-move was made by Herschel V. Johnson of Jefferson County.[3] Johnson had ex-

[1] *Confederate Records of Georgia*, I, 58-156.

[2] Secret meetings were held in Milledgeville on January 24 and January 25, all other meetings there being open. After a recess, meetings were resumed at Savannah, open from March 7 to March 23, closed on March 8, 15, and 21.

[3] As a States' Rights unionist, Johnson had held that North and South should share equally in the territories, and that the territory should decide

pected Alexander Stephens to take the lead in heading off secession. But, on finding that Stephens had concluded that such a move was futile, he took the burden on himself.[4] He offered a preamble and ordinance stating the reasons for Georgia's discontent and proposing to call a meeting at which representatives of the various Southern and border states were to come together in Atlanta in February to discuss relations with the Federal government. If, after resolutions submitted to Congress from this meeting, no redress were to be had, Georgia would go out. There was "an elaborate discussion" on this proposition,[5] after which the previous question was moved and a vote was taken on Johnson's proposal. He lost, but by a fairly close vote—one hundred and sixty-six to one hundred and thirty.[6] Thereupon a committee of seventeen was appointed to frame an ordinance of secession.[7]

It was proposed that the votes received by each delegate to the Convention be made known to the members, and that the ordinance of secession be submitted to a vote of the people. Both proposals were rejected.

The ordinance was brought in from the Committee on January 19 and read twice on motion of Robert Toombs. Calling the union a compact, it repealed the ordinance of the convention of January 2, 1788, which had adopted the Federal Constitution

---

the question of slavery. He insisted on the protection of the South in the Union and bemoaned the split of the Democratic Party in 1860. He was criticized for running as vice-presidential candidate with Stephen Douglas. He was to become president of the Convention in 1865. (Details from *Dictionary of American Biography*.)

[4] P. S. Flippin, *Herschel V. Johnson of Georgia, State Rights Unionist*, pp. 177-179.

[5] By Nisbet, Johnson, T. R. R. Cobb, A. H. Stephens, Toombs, Hill and others.

[6] Later three gentlemen who were absent at the time received permission to vote against it, and one for it, bringing the vote to 169-131.

[7] The Committee consisted of Nisbet, Toombs, Johnson, Jefferson, Barlow, A. H. Stephens, Benning, Williamson, Brown of Macon, Hill of Harris, Rice, Hill of Troup, Trippe, Chastain, Cobb, Colquitt, Kenan, Reese.

and all acts adopting amendments. Benjamin Harvey Hill, supported by both the Stephens brothers, made a last minute effort to save the union by moving that the resolutions of Johnson of the day before be adopted. He lost, in a vote of one hundred thirty-seven to one hundred sixty-four. The minority members of the committee of seventeen voted for the Johnson resolution. [8] The ordinance was carried by a vote of 208 to 89. [9]

Crowds had assembled in Milledgeville to await the decision of the Convention. When the news came that the ordinance had been adopted "the colonial flag of Georgia was raised amidst wild excitement . . . cannon pealed, people shouted and preparations began for the great torchlight procession that night." [10] In contrast, "Herschel V. Johnson . . . and Judge Garnett Andrews . . . darkened their rooms and paced the floor in anguish of heart." [11]

On January 21 when the document was ready for signature, Judge Nisbet proposed that, though there had been difference of opinion on secession, it should be adopted unanimously now that the die had been cast. This was done, [12] but one quasi-protest against the ordinance was offered for the record. [13]

[8] Johnson, Stephens, Williamson, Brown, both Hills, Trippe and Kenan.

[9] One gentleman, absent, later cast an affirmative vote. Among those voting against secession were Johnson and the two Stephens brothers.

[10] L. S. Beeson, *History Stories of Milledgeville and Baldwin County*, p. 49.

[11] *Ibid.*

[12] From the Augusta *Daily Constitutionalist* of January 25 was obtained a picture of the scene that day, at the meeting which had just passed the ordinance of secession and was about to make a new Constitution. It was a "stormy morning . . . the streets are muddy and pedestrian efforts are clogged by an accumulation of pink-aluminous matter, which persons who have not been blessed with reportorial powers are very apt to classify as red clay. . . In the gallery at the capitol it is as dark as a cavern where some few last rays of light have entered in. The members on the floor below appear uncomfortable. . ."

[13] Signed by J. N. Simmons, T. M. McRae, F. H. Latimer, D. Whelchel, P. M. Byrd and James Simmons.

The Convention voted approval of Governor Brown for his prompt action in seizing Fort Pulaski so that a situation similar to that at Fort Sumter might not arise. It authorized him to purchase ships for the use of the State and to make arrangements for communications via the Cuba Telegraph Company. Thanks were given to citizens for allowing the use of their slaves for two weeks at Fort Pulaski and the slaves were paid for their labor.

Standing committees were appointed on: Relations with Slaveholding States of North America; Foreign Relations; Commerce and Postal arrangements; Constitution of the State and the United States. Of these, the ones on Foreign Relations and Constitution bear notice. The Foreign Relations Committee consisted in part of Toombs, A. H. Stephens, Colquitt, H. V. Johnson, and Warner. The Committee on the Constitution was made up in part of T. R. R. Cobb and Linton Stephens. There is no record available of how the committees worked. Beginning with January 22, T. R. R. Cobb, often referred to as the "Constitution-maker," began to submit reports from his committee. More and more he took the lead in dominating the Convention.

Younger brother of Howell Cobb, T. R. R. Cobb had long been a prominent constitutional lawyer and public figure. Supreme Court reporter from 1849 to 1857, he had edited twenty volumes of *Reports* and in 1851 had made a notable *Digest of Georgia Laws*. After Lincoln's election, he agitated for immediate secession, [14] and after the call for the Convention conducted an active campaign in its support. From his outstanding work in framing the Georgia Constitution of 1861, he went on to become chairman of the Committee on a permanent Constitution for the Confederacy, at Montgomery.

Incidental to the consideration of the Constitution were many ordinances, some sorely needed now that Georgia was temporarily acting in an independent and sovereign capacity:

---

14 See his speech in *Confederate Records*, I, 157-182.

Sentences already inflicted should be enforced; more stringent regulations should be made for the trade, immigration, and care of slaves; a postal service should be established; fortifications, and other property formerly belonging to the Union should revert to Georgia; the terms on which citizenship in Georgia might be acquired should be determined as well as the conditions which constituted treason. The former circuit and district courts of the United States would no longer be recognized but be replaced by others. Investments in mines and manufacturing were to be protected, and facilities provided. Georgia would pay its share of the public debt and take its share of the property.

On January 24 the Convention elected delegates to go to Montgomery and take part in forming a confederation of the seceded states. Robert Toombs and Howell Cobb [15] were elected for the State at large. Among the other delegates, who were elected by districts, were E. A. Nisbet, B. H. Hill, T. R. R. Cobb, and A. H. Stephens. These delegates were to commit the State to the Confederation for only twelve months and to propose a form of union acceptable to Georgia.

Before the meeting at Milledgeville closed on January 29, Judge Nisbet read the report—written, he said, by Toombs—of the Committee on the Ordinance of Secession. This report stated the reasons for the separation, and the political philosophy of the secessionists. The primary ground was the interference with the institution of slavery. It was further alleged that the large commercial and manufacturing interests in the North were profiting at the expense of the agricultural interests, and that internal improvements were being made for the

---

[15] Howell Cobb came of a family with money, social position and leadership; it was largely through his power of persuasion that Georgia remained with the Union until after the election of Lincoln. As lawyer, governor, secretary of the treasury, he devoted himself to public affairs. He presided over the meetings at Montgomery. Later he was sent to Georgia to watch events there as the misunderstanding between Governor Brown and Confederate President Jefferson Davis grew. (Details from *Dictionary of American Biography*.)

benefit of monopolistic businesses. Ten thousand copies of this report were ordered printed.

Quite different must have been the spirit of the men who journeyed to old Savannah for the next session. Secession was now a *fait accompli*. The main business of this part of the Convention was to finish the Constitution.

On March 7, election of Jefferson Davis as President of the Confederacy and of A. H. Stephens as Vice-president was approved.

A motion of thanks was voted to R. R. Cuyler, President of the Central Railroad, which had given the delegates free passes to enable them to travel to the Convention. Free return from the Convention was offered by the Georgia Railroad. A steamer trip to Fort Pulaski was provided by the mayor of Savannah, C. C. Jones and Colonel A. R. Lawton, Commandant of the fort.

On March 13, Howell Cobb, President of the Confederate Congress, wired the president of the Convention that a copy of the Confederate Constitution which had been adopted on March 11 was on its way. This copy arrived on March 15, and on March 16, the Confederate Constitution was adopted by a unanimous vote of two hundred and seventy-six. This is reminiscent of the unanimous adoption of the Federal Constitution some seventy-three years earlier.

A few adjustments had to be made as Georgia again took its place in a union. Sale of Confederate bonds was endorsed. The words "United States" were to be replaced in the code of laws by "Confederate States." The governor was authorized to turn over to the Confederacy the forces of the State, which had been individually recruited by officers. Georgia also was prepared to offer ten square miles for a permanent seat of government for the Confederate States.

Realizing that they were probably usurping much authority due to the wartime pressure and the unusual circumstances, these delegates provided that all ordinances which they had passed should be submitted to the General Assembly for modification or repeal except the Ordinance of Secession, and the ratification of the Confederate Constitution.

Finally, on March 21, 1861, the meeting went into secret session on the State Constitution. On March 23, Cobb brought in the final revision, which was passed and signed.[16] For the first time in Georgia's history a Constitution was to be submitted to the people.[17]

President Crawford bade farewell to the delegates in terms indicative of the tone of the meeting:

> Joining in the general opinion, and referring to my own observations of other large deliberative bodies, I venture to say that I have seen none which surpasses this convention in general decorum and all the amenities of social life . . . When first assembled, there was less disagreement as to the burden of our grievances than to their remedy, and especially as to the time of its application.
>
> Happily, conciliation produced concord . . . Clasping each other with a fraternal grasp, they were less intent on sharing in the glory than in participating in common peril and a common destiny. Thus may the sons of Georgia ever be!
>
> You have overturned a government which had become sectional in policy and sectional in hostility. It had lost nationality, and the first requisite of every government—that of protection of person and property. True, you have overthrown the Federal Union, but you have preserved the Federal Constitution . . . in short, you have effected a political reformation.
>
> Like your ancestors, you commenced with a few leading ideas or principles. They may be epitomized thus: a right, when assailed, must be either defended or surrendered. . . . The alternative of the first proposition you have chosen. . . .

---

[16] Original copies of this Constitution, as well as those of 1865, 1868, 1877, may be read in the records of the Conventions.

[17] The vote for ratification was 11,499 to 10,704, a majority of only 795. The total vote was only 22,203 out of a possible vote of 120,000. (Details from I. W. Avery, *History of Georgia*, p. 207).

In the revision of your State Constitution, you have, in my judgment, improved it by each alteration . . . Whatever may have been heretofore the high standard of your judges, that standard will be advanced still higher to independence and legal attainments. Reduction of the members of the Legislature may not have gone as far as many others have desired; still as a thing, *per se,* it cannot be otherwise than acceptable. In all such matters we must make concessions.

# CHAPTER XI
# THE CONSTITUTION OF 1861

## I. Fundamental Principles

The Constitution of 1861 contained Georgia's first formal Declaration of Fundamental Principles. It was also the first to be submitted to the people for ratification. Property qualifications had already been abolished by amendments, and the recall principle had been adopted for many officials. Popular control was greatly advanced by all these innovations.

The Confederate Constitution had just been adopted by the Convention. The new Georgia Constitution was to bring the State into line with the new union. The earnest men of the Convention tried to guarantee the rights of the people of Georgia within the new union.

Among the fundamental principles, and reminiscent of the Declaration of Independence which preceded formal entry into the Federal Union, was the statement that the forms of government

> may be altered or modified whenever the safety or happiness of the governed requires it. No government should be changed for light or transient causes; nor unless upon reasonable assurance that a better will be established. Protection to person and property is the duty of government.

In addition to old principles were safeguards requiring that every person charged with an offense must not only have a trial by jury, but must be furnished with a copy of the charges, be confronted with witnesses against him and have a compulsory process for obtaining his own witnesses; no person might be put on trial more than once for the same offense; no conviction might work corruption of blood or forfeiture of estate; the power of the court to punish for contempt must be limited by legislative Acts.

For the first time, judicial review received official recognition—"Legislative Acts in violation of the fundamental law are void; and the Judiciary shall so declare them."[1] There were clauses protecting the obligation of contract; declaring that laws must have a general operation and laying the grounds upon which, alone, taxation might be imposed. New, too, was the provision that no right of way might be granted by the State or any of its subdivisions except for public use, and then only upon just compensation in advance.

## II. Few Changes in the Three Departments

For the first time, compensation for members of the General Assembly was provided. Additional restrictions were placed upon the granting by the legislature of corporate powers. The legislature might grant no such powers to private companies except in the case of those engaged in banking, insurance, railroad, canal, plank road, navigation, mining, express, lumber and telegraph. No law might be passed which would compel a citizen, directly or indirectly, to become a stockholder in, or to contribute to, a railroad or other internal improvement, except in a corporate town or city. The power of taxation was not limited when it came to making levees or dams to prevent floods.

All elections were to be by ballot. Judges of both the Supreme and the Superior Court were appointive. The terms of Supreme Court judges were to be fixed by the legislature. Superior Court judges were to hold office four years.[2]

---

[1] The word "shall" gives force to the power, since it seems to connote "must" rather than simply "may". An examination of the cases tried will indicate that this was the interpretation put upon this section by the judiciary and accepted in practice.

[2] The Constitution of 1865 restored the election of judges of the Supreme Court with six year terms to the legislature. It gave the election of Superior Court judges with four year terms to circuits.

The Constitution of 1868 invested the governor again with the right of appointment of all judges. Those in the Supreme Court had terms of twelve years, Superior Court eight years. The jurisdiction was not materially changed.

### III. Miscellaneous Provisions

Besides reference to the "Confederate States" three other references were made to the circumstances making necessary this Constitution: electors must be "free white males"; all officers should continue and all laws should operate until this new Constitution was in force; the Revised Code which was adopted by the last legislature was to be altered to specify "Confederate States".

### IV. How the Constitution was Applied

Only eleven thousand four hundred ninety-nine votes were cast for the Constitution of 1861, while ten thousand seven hundred and four were against it.[3] The thoughts of war already weighed heavily on the people. Governor Joseph E. Brown, assuming war powers, had already taken preliminary measures to safeguard the State. Further provisions were made, for example, for the regulation of whiskey, and the limitation of cotton acreage to three acres, with violation subject to a fine of $500 per acre.[4] An income tax measure and a sales tax were passed.[5] Conflict arose between Governor Brown and the Confederacy over the rights of the State in matters of conscription, exemptions, appointment and *habeas corpus*.

The Constitution could not have been tested in war as it would have been in peace. Following 1859 there was a period of silence on constitutional questions.

---

Thus, during the Civil War and Reconstruction period there is a vacillation of policy in regard to the selection of judges, which may have been a reflection of the unsettled conditions. The Constitution of 1877 provided for election of judges by the General Assembly, but that of 1945 gave the election to the people.

3 An early historian gives as the reason for the light vote on the new Constitution the fact that the people were already absorbed in war. Avery, *op. cit.*, p. 207.

4 Coulter, *op. cit.*, p. 306.

5 *Ibid*, p. 315.

From 1861 to 1866 the United States District Courts were in "innocuous desuetude." [6] By ordinance of Convention, January 25, 1861, Georgia abolished the circuit and district courts of the United States for the district of Georgia, and established "the district courts of the Independent State of Georgia." The Confederacy, when organized, had no Supreme Court. The Georgia Superior and Supreme Courts upheld the jurisdiction of the Confederate Court for the District of Georgia and its personnel behaved with "dignity and power." [7] The types of cases handled were largely sequestration cases, those involving seizure of vessels, alien property, counterfeit, and matters pertaining to the dissolution of former partnerships. [8]

From 1859 to 1865, cases of various types came before the Supreme Court of Georgia, but in very few of them were issues of constitutionality involved. There was a *habeas corpus* case (1862) [9] in which the right of the Congress of the Confederate States to provide for the public defense was upheld. [10]

A decision in 1864 [11] declared: "no person is exempt from fighting by reason of having furnished a substitute." The Act of 1862, challenged on *habeas corpus* grounds, had provided for calling out men for three years. It was defended on the basis of the Federal Constitution of which "our constitution . . . is a liberal copy"; "the experience which induced its adoption was our experience". Two cases were involved. Three men who had employed substitutes (in accordance with a law passed on April 16, 1862) were summoned for service under an act passed in 1864. Two sued in Macon on the ground of

[6] *Georgia Historical Quarterly*, IX (1925) Warren Grice "The Confederate States' Court for Georgia", pp. 131-158.

[7] Grice, *op. cit.*, p. 158.

[8] Robinson, *Justice in Grey*, p. 228.

[9] Jeffers *v.* Fair, 33 *Ga.* 347 (1862). Chief Justice Taney and President Lincoln were having similar problems. (Ex Parte Merryman, 17 Federal Cases, 144; Ex parte Milligan, 4 Wallace 2).

[10] Act of April 16, 1862, amended September 27, 1862.

[11] 38 *Ga.* (Supplement) (1864).

violation of contract and lost; one sued in Atlanta and won. The cases then came to the Supreme Court, where Judge Jenkins declared the later law constitutional. An exemption is not a contract and "no legislature can divest itself or its successor of any power necessary to the well being of the state."

In 1865, there was a test case on war-power and drafting for service other than military. It involved an Act of 1864 [12] which had provided that the age limit for the army, by Confederate law, should be seventeen to fifty; for those unable to serve except in some light work, it should be eighteen to forty-five. Two men brought suit on *habeas corpus* grounds, but the act was found constitutional. A reservation, however, was expressed by Judge Jenkins:

> War power is liable to abuse . . . and taking into view . . . the complicated nature of international affairs, unavoidably imperiling the peace of nations, the vast armies employed in modern warfare, and the tendency to encroachment of political power in free governments, we see clearly that a proper adjustment of the latter is a problem by no measure easy of solution.[13]

The number of cases arising under this Constitution was comparatively small. They involved such constitutional issues as trial by jury, *habeas corpus*,[14] jurisdiction of inferior courts,[15] and the right to bear weapons.[16]

[12] 34 *Ga.* 136 (1865).

[13] Two of Georgia's outstanding lawyers took opposite sides in this case, Howell Cobb representing the plaintiffs, Linton Stephens the defendants.

[14] Taylor *v.* Jeter 33 *Ga.* 195 (January 1862).

[15] Chapman *v.* Woodruff 34 *Ga.* 91 (November 1864).

[16] Stockdale *v.* State 32 *Ga.* 227 (January 1861).

# CHAPTER XII
# THE CONSTITUTION OF 1865

## I. THE CONVENTION

When the war closed, the reins of government in Georgia were held at first by General Wilson; later James Johnson was appointed Provisional Governor. On July 13, the latter issued a call for a constitutional convention to be held on October 25.

An election for delegates to the convention was held on October 4, 1865. The meeting in the Hall of Representatives at Milledgeville was solemn and important, for this Convention had the task of framing a Constitution acceptable to the United States. It was a conservative group, much less brilliant than the secession convention. Elected by people who must take an amnesty oath before voting, some of the delegates themselves were unpardoned when elected. Of the delegates

> twenty-two had been delegates to the secession convention of 1861, and all but one had voted against secession on the test resolution. Fourteen who had been defeated candidates for the 1861 convention on an anti-secession platform were elected in 1865. Very few chosen in 1865 were known as strong secessionists and few had been thorough-going unionists during the war. The great majority had disapproved of immediate secession, had voted the Bell-Everett or the Douglas-Johnson ticket in 1860 and had then gone with the state when war actually came and a great many had served in the army.[1]

The *Daily Constitutionalist* of Augusta had a special correspondent on the scene at Milledgeville, and published on November 1, 1865, an account of a session of the Convention. The date was October 28, the place, the Hall of the House of Representatives,

> an apartment very inconvenient . . . for so large an assemblage—so inconvenient, in fact, that probably taking the

---

[1] C. M. Thompson, *Reconstruction in Georgia*, p. 148.

front from the galleries, where spectators sit with hats on as though at a cock-pit, a member yesterday introduced a resolution to allow members to sit covered! Over the Presidential seat is a full length portrait of his excellency Governor James Jackson, of Georgia, the man who " burned the Yazoo fraud with fire from Heaven " . . . To the right of the chair is a portrait, also full length, of Benjamin Franklin, clad in knee breeches and Quaker brown, and smiling affably on an electric machine: to the left is a life size presentment of the Marquis de la Fayette . . . Here close to the chair is Mr. Joshua Hill, tall, strong looking, determined, with knitted brows, spectacled eyes, and steely gray beard poring over a newspaper, but still with eye and ear both open to what is going on. A very Boanerges in debate, Mr. Hill has been so stoutly met by some other members as to have made such occasional encounters most entertaining . . . persistently in the minority . . . Next to this gentleman is Mr. Jenkins,[2] grave, venerable, composed, listened to at times in the deepest silence . . . Mr. Seward . . . tooth and nail against the war debt, Mr. Cohen . . . who made a beautiful speech in favor of petitioning the release of Mr. Davis . . .

The leaders of the previous convention—Toombs, the Stephens brothers, the Cobbs, Hill, and Brown were absent. Both the right to amnesty and the right to participation in State affairs were denied to civil officers of the Confederate government, military officers above the rank of colonel, naval officers above the rank of lieutenant, governors, congressmen, judges, West Point officers, and citizens worth more than twenty thousand dollars. For these groups individual pardons must be obtained from the President of the United States.

[2] C. J. Jenkins—An ardent union Whig at the Convention of 1850, he wrote the resolutions for the Georgia Platform. He deprecated the drift toward secession. Appointed to the Georgia Supreme Court, he served during the whole war. He declined the presidency of the Constitutional Convention of 1865 but was chairman of the Committee on Business. He opposed the 14th amendment. As reconstruction governor he challenged and defied Congressional reconstruction. He served as president of the Constitutional Convention of 1877.

## THE CONSTITUTION OF 1865

Only two outstanding pre-war men were present, Charles J. Jenkins and Herschel V. Johnson. Johnson was elected president of the meeting. In that capacity he conducted himself admirably. In his *Autobiography*, he said that his policy was to abstain from politics, and that the "concessions to the victorious show how earnestly the vanquished in a gallant and patriotic struggle sought harmony and peace." [3]

The tone of the meeting was set by the election of Herschel V. Johnson as president of the Convention. Johnson, a man of honesty and integrity, who, in the old Union had been a partisan of states' rights in the Confederacy, opposed conscription as a violation of states' rights. He had introduced an amendment to the Confederate Constitution permitting peaceful secession, and he had opposed the suspension of the writ of *habeas corpus* and the establishment of a Confederate Supreme Court. [4] The sentiment evinced by this Convention was in keeping with Johnson's principles: the rights of the State were asserted, yet cooperation with the new regime was furthered.

After the amnesty oath was administered, the first important business was to repeal the Ordinance of Secession. The word "repeal" was deliberately chosen—not the word "annul". The war was over, the secession ordinance had served its purpose, and it was repealed. But the right to secede was in no sense denied by annulment.

It was decided that a committee of sixteen, one from each judicial circuit, could best steer the work of the Convention, and such a committee was appointed. Thereafter all business was referred to this committee. The chairman was Jenkins. [5]

A message from the governor highlighted the first day's session. He enumerated the troubles the State was having as

[3] Flippen, *op. cit.*, p. 269.
[4] Summary from *Dictionary of American Biography*.
[5] The other members were: D. Irwin, J. C. Nichols, A. H. Chappell, J. F. B. Jackson, R. A. T. Ridley, E. G. Cabaniss, C. B. Cole, W. M. Reese, A. H. Kenan, J. L. Wimberly, J. L. Seward, Henry Morgan, W. F. Wright, T. C. Lloyd, J. P. Simmons.

it entered upon the post-war era. The cotton purchased by the State had been captured or burned, and all assets abroad had been fully drawn against. The State-owned Western and Atlantic Railroad was yielding no income. It had been seized and kept by the United States until September 25. Since that time, on the governor's authority, some repairs had been made and nine engines and a hundred cars had been bought from the United States, but shops, cross-ties, iron, and bridges were still needed.

The governor said, furthermore, that he had borrowed for mileage and per diem pay for the members of the Convention. Stock in banks and other railroads was unavailable. Charitable institutions were without funds. The penitentiary and shops were nearly destroyed; the convicts had escaped or were discharged. Such was the dark picture presented to the delegates. Two recommendations the governor suggested for immediate action: the Supreme Court should be independent of the executive, and should sit at the seat of the government; and the question of debts must be settled. The public debt of the State was $20,813,525. The pre-war debt of the State must be met ($2,667,750). That created during the war, ($18,135,775), "of no legal or moral obligation", being unconstitutional, must be extinguished. He urged that they not refer the matter to the legislature, which would have enough to do with taxes, police, penal situations, and contracts, but that they settle the matter themselves. The governor averred that if left alone, Georgia would be able to work out its own salvation. At a later point in the session, extensive accounts were given, by Ex-Governor Brown, of the cotton confiscated during the war, and reports were made on finances in general.

Various ordinances were passed by the Convention. The property of debtors was exempted from levy and sale until the first session of the next legislature. Governor Johnson was authorized to borrow on the credit of the State to pay the civil list until sufficient taxes could be raised; he was authorized to borrow for the Western and Atlantic Railroad. Private contracts, expressed or implied, entered into during the war were made valid; so, too, were renewals of those made before the commencement of hostilities. Further ordinances designed to bring stability were those legalizing contracts made by guardians for freedmen and freedwomen; providing for widows and orphans of deceased soldiers, and for disabled soldiers; and making valid all acts passed since January 18, 1861, not in conflict with the Constitution of the United States or with the State Constitution. The legislature was requested not to multiply offices and expenses.

The sense of insecurity that prevailed at this time is shown in two resolutions—one calling upon the governor to provide one or more militia companies in every county, for want of an adequate police force; one urging that a committee of five men [6] be instructed to draw up a code for freedmen. The General Assembly would, of course, have to take appropriate action in these matters.

President Andrew Johnson was requested to restore the State to the Union as speedily as possible, amd to pardon those who had been excluded from the previous amnesty proclamation.

The most controversial task of the Convention was the repudiation of the war debt. On November 8, the day of adjournment, repudiation was voted after much argument, and only after insistance by President Johnson and William H. Seward that this action was absolutely necessary.

On November 15, 1865, the *Augusta Daily Constitutionalist* turned its wrath against repudiation. A "propulsion of misunderstood telegrams, the pressure of unauthorized threats, the fancied sight of uplifted sword passed the ordinance"; "the Convention was the gun and a Federal hand pulled the trigger"; "in no fair sense was there a majority vote at Milledgeville"; —such were the charges of the editor. The editorial gave an analysis of the situation. The number of delegates was

6 E. Starnes, L. Stephens, W. Hull, L. E. Bleckley, L. H. Whittbe.

three hundred. The vote on repudiation was two hundred and fifty of which one hundred and seventeen were nays, and one hundred and thirty-three yeas. Nearly one half of the entire negative vote came from thirty-seven wealthy and well-populated counties. Those voting against it included "judges, soldiers, advocates, editors, physicians, planters"; "wherever were found wealth, population, railroads, schools, post-offices, journals, there you found the nays;" "from out-lying and sparsely peopled districts that, by means of a faulty system, outvote three to one, in legislative halls, ten times their population and twenty times their wealth were found the yeas." As before, the older section of the State found it hard to lose to the up-country.

The people ratified the Constitution by a vote of seventeen thousand six hundred and ninety-nine. In the election for governor, Charles J. Jenkins was elected without opposition with thirty-seven thousand two hundred votes. Why the vote for the Constitution was so much smaller than that for governor is not clear. The seeming apathy was justified in the occurrences of the next few years.

On December 19, Governor Jenkins was inaugurated and recognized by the United States Government. The legislature assembled on January 15, 1866, and on April 2 news came that the President had proclaimed peace. Congress was not satisfied and presented the Fourteenth Amendment for adoption as a condition of readmission. In November, 1866, at the meeting of the legislature, this became the major issue. Georgia refused to ratify the amendment, and Congress resorted to reconstruction. The Constitution which Georgia had ratified was rejected. For this reason, it seems futile to dwell long on the Constitution of 1865.

## II. THE CONSTITUTION ITSELF

The Constitution of 1865 retained the framework of that of 1861. The Declaration of Fundamental Principles was kept, being retained under the name of a Declaration of Rights; it was preceded by a Preamble almost identical with that of the Constitution of the United States. The legislature was given the right to grant the power of taxation, for designated purposes, to county authorities and municipal corporations; thus the sphere of home rule was enlarged. While acquiescing in the action of the government of the United States in the abolition of slavery, it was stated that compensation was expected for loss sustained.[7] The rights of free persons of color (those with one-eighth Negro blood) were to be provided by statute:[8] property rights, testimony in courts, marriage relations, inheritance and wills, immigration into the State and procedure in civil and criminal suits.[9]

The General Assembly was authorized to provide for general education and to restore the State University.[10] Electors were

[7] They were perhaps thinking of the precedent set by England or the compensated emancipation proposals previously made in the United States.

[8] On December 19, 1865, the legislature followed this up with certain laws for the freedmen, granting the legal rights to sue and to testify except in cases where whites were parties. They were not to serve on juries, or vote.

[9] In 1899, the Georgia Bar Association raised the question: "Are Courts Responsible for Lynchings, and if so why?" An Act of 1866 allowed the judge to call Special Sessions of the Superior Courts to try criminals (in 1890 this was amended to cover civil cases as well); until then lynchings were unheard of. The point taken by the Bar Association was that the Act of 1866 was passed to meet the needs growing out of the new citizenships but that it had the effect of depriving the court of its "mantle of unchangeableness". Its purpose was to relieve the counties of the expense of keeping all the new prisoners who could not afford bond and needed a quick trial; but this paved the way for lack of respect for the law. An era of lynchings reflected the changes.

[10] In December 1866 an education committee of sixteen in the house, and a similar committee in the senate, presented a plan to go into effect on January 1, 1868. The system was to include a State school superintendent, a county commissioner for each county and three trustees in each district, to have charge of the public schools. The schools were to be free to all whites from six to twenty-one and disabled or indigent soldiers under thirty. They were to be supported by county tax and a share of the State funds (Thompson, *op. cit.*, p. 121). Congressional reconstruction came and

134   A CONSTITUTIONAL HISTORY OF GEORGIA

"free white male citizens". [11]

Since 1865 it has been considered unnecessary to include the provision: [12]

> the marriage relation between white persons and persons of African descent, is forever prohibited and such marriage shall be null and void, and it shall be the duty of the General Assembly to enact laws for the punishment of any officer who shall knowingly issue a license for the celebration of such marriage, and any officer or minister of the gospel who shall marry such persons together.

---

the plan was deferred until 1873. It is clear, however, that the public school system was not the result of the reconstruction regime, since the seeds were sown prior to the 1868 convention.

[11] Florida and South Carolina made the same provision at this time. F. N. Thorpe, *op. cit.*

[12] Marriage between Negroes was legalized by act of the legislature and parental responsibility fixed.

# CHAPTER XIII
# THE RECONSTRUCTION CONSTITUTION
## I. The Convention of 1867-1868

Upon the refusal of Georgia to accede to the Fourteenth Amendment, it was reduced to a military regime under the Reconstruction Acts of March 2 and March 23, 1867. General Pope controlled the third Military District, (Georgia, Alabama and Florida) from April, 1867 to January, 1868, followed by General Meade until July 30, 1868, when the army was withdrawn. Radical reconstruction necessitated a new Constitution. Delegates to the convention, consisting of white people sworn by an ironclad oath, and Negroes, could be counted upon to ratify the Fourteenth Amendment. A constitutional point was involved here. If Georgia had never been out of the union, it could not be forced into a vote. If it had been and still was, why was it necessary to obtain a ratification upon a constitutional question?

Many Georgia people felt that since the State was in an anomalous position, it would be better not to register. Herschel V. Johnson urged people to register, then vote against a constitutional convention. To some it seemed that not to register would throw the State into the hands of the Negroes, carpetbaggers and scalawags who would gladly sell their votes for what they would fetch. The registration officials were paid twenty-six cents for each name enrolled.[1] Ex-Governor Brown advised people to vote for a convention.

In 1867 General Pope got the machinery for registration started, dividing the State into forty-seven districts, in each of which was a board of registrars consisting of two whites and one Negro. The process of registration took all summer and until October 1. After registration an election was to be held at which it would be decided whether or not there should be a

---

[1] Thompson, *op. cit.*, p. 186.

convention, and if so, who should serve as delegates. [2] The total registration came to 188,671, of which 95,214 were whites, 93,457 Negroes. [3] Between October 29 and November 2, 1867, the election was held, the vote for a convention carrying by 102,283 out of a total vote of 106,410. [4]

Historians and contemporaries vary in their opinions on the Convention of 1867-1868. One writer described it as a group of "puppets, and harlequins." [5] Other realized that Georgia was forced to decide among three possible courses— meeting Congress half-way, committing suicide by giving in, and sitting silently by in utter defeatism. That it chose the first, and met without disorder the conditions imposed, it speaks well for the temper of the people. There was no violent outbreak, no race warfare, only a dignified business-like attitude. The Convention represented conquest, disfranchisement of leaders, and the seating of Negroes. The political complexion was republican. The leaders, though not native Georgians, were long-time residents—men like Rufus B. Bullock, Benjamin Conley, Foster Blodgett, J. E. Bryant (of the Freedmen's Bureau), C. H. Prince, A. L. Harris, A. T. Ackerman, H. K. McKay. These were assisted and abetted by the leading Negroes, A. A. Bradley, [6] T. G. Campbell and H. M. Turner. [7] With the exception of Bradley, who was a nuisance, consistently raising the question of "Point of Order", and swaggering,

2 Details from W. A. Dunning, *Essays on Civil War and Reconstruction*, pp. 186-191.

3 Cited from C. B. Gosnell, *Government and Politics in Georgia*, p. 33.

4 Cited from Thompson, *op. cit.*, p. 189.

5 Avery, *op. cit.*, p. 376.

6 Bradley was expelled in the course of the meeting on February 12, 1868. Even the *Daily New Era* expressed satisfaction at this point. He was proved to have been convicted of felony in New York. Campbell had a bad reputation for stirring up trouble in his own neighborhood. Turner had been chaplain of a Negro regiment in the war. He remained to carry on his work after the reconstruction period was over.

7 Details from Thompson, *op. cit.*, and *Daily New Era*.

## THE RECONSTRUCTION CONSTITUTION 137

the Negroes were well-behaved and cooperative, voting consistently with the radical republicans.

On December 20, 1867, the *Daily Constitutionalist* of Augusta published [8] an account of the opening meeting of the Convention. Here was the scene depicted by an eye-witness:

> In a small room located in the City Hall . . . today was enacted the prologue to the drama or farce which will be on the boards for the next six or eight weeks. The room itself is worthy of the use to which it has been devoted, being small and shabby, and furnished with an abundance of pine desks painted brown, and reed bottomed chairs, the very picture of hard times; to say nothing of the wooden ink stands and cheap stationery, together with the green calico of different shades of color which covers the long glass windows at the back of the President's chair. Taken as a whole, a most melancholy air pervades the apartment, strongly suggestive, indeed, of the garret on Broadway in which the "ghouls" occasionally meet to expound their religious doctrines. There are no galleries, no places for spectators save except a small space at the further end of the room which has been railed off, and which by hard squeezing might be made to hold about seventy persons.
>
> It might have been about nine o'clock in the morning when the delegates began to assemble in their funereal looking hall. At first the number was small, and the few present grouped around the stove that stood between the first row of benches and the President's chair, and discussed politics. Without exaggerating, I can say that a more seedy looking body of men never assembled together in Georgia. As the men warmed themselves around the stove, the scene was decidedly rich. Unshaven, uncombed, unwashed, and in most cases, very dirtily dressed, stood and sat the legislators of the State, deep in conversation, which was only interrupted by the continuous squirting of tobacco juice into small tin spittoons, of which there are over two hundred scattered over the room . . .

[8] From Atlanta, December 9, by "special correspondent" of the New York *Herald*.

No Negroes had yet entered the Convention Hall, but a step across to the room opposite discovered the presence of some thirty or more sable delegates, who had thus assembled together, probably because they were ashamed of being seen in the company of their white colleagues. They formed a motley and interesting gathering. From the light yellow mulatto to the coal black African, and from the obsequious barber to the sturdy cotton picker, there they were as large as life, and carrying themselves with a dignity and air of importance at once ludicrous and pitiful—a few out of the number are able to read and write; the majority are as innocent of all educational qualities as a babe of three weeks old. A single glance at this body of Negroes will tell you how utterly farcical must be a convention which contains such members.

The meeting then assembled at ten o'clock and the account continues:

Had a stranger, ignorant of the purpose for which the men present had been convened, arrived at the moment, he would never have supposed that a State Constitutional Convention was being then called to order.

To summarize the next part of the account, Mr. G. W. "Ashman" (the record gives "Ashburn") called the Convention to order and nominated Foster Blodgett temporary chairman. The ayes were called for, whereupon it was announced that the motion was carried. A delegate then called for the noes of which there was a storm. A pause ensued, then a discussion, and Blodgett was declared elected. "Higby" (the record gives "Bigby") was nominated as temporary secretary. A Negro member nominated another, whereupon "Bradley, the Boston negro lawyer and Radical firebrand of Georgia, made a brief speech opposing the nominations." "Ashman" looked perplexed at the members and they at him. Three minutes passed. It was a "really laughable tableau," when "with a deep sigh, Ashman descended from the stand leaving neither chairman nor sec-

## THE RECONSTRUCTION CONSTITUTION 139

retary." The white spectators smiled. Finally a member proposed that a committee conduct Blodgett to the chair. The Convention then proceeded to business.

This was the first Constitutional Convention held in Atlanta, so recently burned and rebuilt. The physical condition of the Hall in which the delegates met was bad. The messenger was authorized to put up shades at the window on the east side; a clock was purchased and the broken lights were replaced in the windows on the north end. The messenger was instructed to ventilate the place each day by opening the upper sections of the windows. He must furnish water and purchase fuel and lights. The porter, Charles Potterman, was paid five dollars a day (from which he had to pay for any assistance) for which his duties were to make fires, bring water, sweep, and keep the hall in order.[9]

The major problems of the Convention were the Fourteenth Amendment, the qualifications of the electorate, debts, the relief of debtors, and allocation of powers to the various departments.

In his introductory remarks as temporary president, Foster Blodgett struck the keynote. Many, he said, "cling to the ruins of a structure that now belongs to the past;" those who "controlled affairs of the South precipitated the result of a vain effort to wrest these plantation States from the Union." The problem now was to go forward, not to look backward. There was need to provide for the wants of a great community, to regulate supply and demand, to frame legislation so as to relieve the pressing wants of agricultural and commercial classes. The major problem, as he painted it, was the need for relief from debts. The wealthy agricultural class was reduced to poverty. Domestic industry was changed. The system of reckon-

---

9 Atlanta, from this time on, was destined to be the seat of government. The Constitution of 1861 had provided that it should be and had authorized the Assembly to provide for the erection of a Capitol and other public buildings. This had not been done at the time of the Constitutional Convention of 1877. At that time, it was decided that Atlanta should be the Capital if the people agreed. This ordinance was attached as a separate provision and not part of the fundamental law.

ing capital in lands and labor was gone. The price of cotton was low, and great depression was reflected in all kinds of business. Furthermore, the needs of education, both lower and higher, must be met. Nothing, he said, could be done until reconstruction was accomplished. He urged that the two races live in harmony. As Bullock put it, the motto of the convention would be "wisdom, justice, moderation."

J. R. Parrott, permanent president, said in his inaugural speech:

> Many of us have come here from amongst a people who have spurned us and spit upon us, simply because we have advocated the settlement of the questions which have torn asunder the ties of friendship . . . We should form a State Government, for an unwilling people.

In spite of the difficulties, Parrott urged that they make a fundamental law of which Georgia might be proud.

The early days of the meeting were wasted on the introduction of so many various ordinances and resolutions, that finally, on December 16, a special committee of ten was appointed to determine the function and power of the convention.[10] On the same day, the work of the delegates was parcelled among sixteen standing committees: On Privileges and Elections, Petitions, Enrollment, Journals, Finances, Printing, Auditing, Bill of Rights, Franchise, Legislative Department, Executive Department, Judiciary Department, Education, Militia, Relief, Revision. Of these committees, those on Bill of Rights, Franchise, Relief and Revision were probably outstanding.[11]

---

[10] The committee consisted of H. K. McKay, F. Blodgett, W. P. Hotchkiss, J. H. Caldwell, H. V. M. Miller, R. H. Whiteley, B. Conley, W. Shropshire, J. L. Dunning, A. T. Akerman.

[11] The committee on Bill of Rights consisted of G. W. Ashburn, C. P. Davis, W. T. Crane, W. L. Marler, A. G. Foster, C. H. Hopkins, L. L. Stanford. The committee on Franchise was composed of J. E. Bryant, W. Shropshire, N. L. Angier, P. B. Bedford, E. S. Cobb, P. Yeates, J. L. Dunning. The committee on Relief was made up of: J. Harris, W. W. Dews, W. L. Goodwin, W. H. Whitehead, T. P. Saffold, R. B. Bullock,

A picture of the Convention of 1867-1868 may be obtained from the pages of the *Atlanta Daily New Era*. On December 12, 1867, this paper, siding with the minority, expressed in an editorial its approval of the Convention. It railed at the "disgraceful" tenor of the news articles. On the tenth of December, the day after the assembling of the meeting, the *New Era* said "we need not counsel the Convention as to the course it ought to pursue. Its business is prominately, (sic) before it and the landmarks of the past are up as its guide;" "wholesome, dignified, undiscriminating action is what is needed;" "prejudices, ill-will, memories of ancient wrong and all lingering thirst for revenge should be put far away, and only the good of the whole people be allowed to influence the actions." Yet the general tone of this same paper is characterized by vindictiveness and spite.[12]

Most of the journals [13] dubbed the Convention the "Unconstitutional Convention", but not the *New Era*. On January 16, after the Christmas recess, it commented: "the opposition party thought they had the thing dead, that further legislation by the convention would go by default," but on the contrary, it would proceed characterized by "quietude", "self-confidence", "readiness and disposition for work"; "the delegates have returned from their constituencies with their minds made up as to what the people demand." On January 18 it said:

> Opposition to all action by the Convention, on the part of the press of Georgia, demonstrates one fact to our mind: That is, the papers have set out with the cold determination to oppose the convention right or wrong.

---

A. T. Akerman. The members of the Revision Committee were: H. V. M. Miller, J. Harris, G. W. Ashburn, A. T. Akerman, H. K. McKay, J. H. Caldwell, J. S. Bigby, J. E. Bryant.

[12] As witness the publication for the "sake of amusement" of the Georgia daily press comments when Governor Jenkins and Treasurer Jones were removed.

[13] Atlanta *Daily Intelligence* January 16, 1868, Griffin, *Tri-Weekly Star*, January 30, and others.

Not all the vituperative journalism was on one side. One instance of this sort of thing on the other side will suffice. The Relief Bill was up for debate on January 27. The question was whether or not there should be collection of debts incurred prior to June 1, 1865. A. Alpeoria Bradley, the Negro leader, "after some characteristic points with the President, asserting his right to the floor, addressed himself particularly to his colored friends. He said many white members had called upon and asked him and his colored friends to support them in the Relief question, they (the whites) would support them on other questions." Among others Mr. McCay (later Justice) spoke in favor of relief. The Griffin *Tri-Weekly Star* of January 30 said that he "disgraced himself by saying public opinion forced him into the Confederate service." "Oh Shame!" the *Star* went on; "what a pity that a man should lack moral courage and nerve enough to live four years of his life a hypocrite and deceiver."

The apparent sycophancy of the delegates, and the tone of subserviency in messages of thanks to the United States for its magnanimity, and for the Freedmen's Bureau, have been criticized. In fairness to the members, it may be said that perhaps this was no false humility. Given an opportunity to serve for the first time, one might conceivably be grateful for the chance. It is, indeed, surprising how little there was of bluster, and the Constitution produced bears favorable comparison with other Georgia Constitutions. Whatever fights occurred were not between radical Republicans and conservative Democrats, but between radical and conservative Republicans. This is evidenced by differences of opinion on relief between Bullock and Akerman, and in majority and minority reports. The debates on the Constitution began in earnest about January 15, and continued until March 11, when it was adopted by a vote of one hundred and eighteen to thirteen. Thirty-four members were absent.[14]

---

[14] There appear to be several unaccounted for, besides Bradley, who had been expelled. The president obtained permission to cast his vote in the affirmative.

# THE RECONSTRUCTION CONSTITUTION 143

Beginning on December 20, 1867, the question of payment of the expenses of the Convention became urgent. John Jones, State treasurer, refused to appropriate money unless authorized by the governor. The governor, Charles Jenkins, said he could not authorize this expenditure, which was to have been met by a special tax levied for the purpose. General Pope ordered him to authorize it anyway. He consistently refused. Thus the matter stood when General Pope was removed and General Meade succeeded him on December 28. On January 7, 1868 General Meade ordered the governor to authorize the disbursement of the money. Again he refused. The general dismissed both the governor and the treasurer, setting up General T. H. Ruger as military governor. Governor Jenkins left the State, taking with him for safekeeping $400,000 and the State seal. He proceeded to Washington to file suit to test the case in the Supreme Court. He had twice already filed suits there in protest against Reconstruction Acts.[15]

Provision was made for the submission of the Constitution to a vote and for the election of officers, on April 30. On March 11 the Ordinance of Secession, the act adopting the Confederate Constitution, and all acts between January 16 and March 24, 1861, were repealed[16] and the war debt was repudiated, thus re-affirming the actions of the Convention of 1865. On the same day, an ordinance was passed that the Convention might reconvene at any time in twelve months to complete the reconstruction of the State.[17] To assure Georgia's re-entry into the Union, provision was made that

> the State of Georgia shall ever remain a member of the American union; the people thereof are a part of the American nation; every citizen thereof owes paramount allegiance to the Constitution and government of the United States and no

15 6 Wallace 50; 6 Wallace 241. See *Chapter XIV*.

16 Note that they were not annulled.

17 Such completion became necessary, but it was not done at the hands of the Convention.

law or ordinance of this State, in contravention or subversion thereof, shall ever have any binding force.

At the time designated, Georgia ratified the Constitution by 89,007 to 71,309.[18] R. B. Bullock was elected governor.

Authorities have generally agreed that the reconstruction Constitution was sound in its fundamental principles. It gave too much leeway for debtors and homestead, and extended to the Assembly too much power to grant to towns and cities the right to tax or vote stock in corporations. The Constitution was not at fault, perhaps, but the human beings who were charged with its administration, subject as they were to the influences of an age of over-speculation and investment.

## II. THE CONSTITUTION

Here, then, is the product of the Convention. Let it speak for itself. In the Declaration of Fundamental Principles, Georgia conformed to the amendments to the Constitution of the United States in renouncing slavery and involuntary servitude. Having previously passed an act forbidding the marriage relationship between Negro and white, it added, to the fundamental law not subject to legislation, the provision that "the social status of the citizen shall never be the subject of legislation." [19]

Concern for social and humanitarian reforms was expressed in the provisions that imprisonment for debt and whipping as a punishment for crime, should be outlawed. No lottery was to be authorized, and no poll-tax might be levied except for educational purposes. Mechanics and laborers were to have liens upon the property of their employers for labor or material furnished. A section on duelling made any man ineligible to vote

[18] The Florida vote on a Constitution of 1868 was 14,520 - 9,491. That of North Carolina was 93,118 - 74,009; of South Carolina, 70,558 - 27,288; Virginia, after rejecting clauses in regard to a test oath and disenfranchisement, ratified the remainder in 1870 by 210,585 - 9,136. Thorpe, *op. cit.*

[19] Even though the Civil War settled the question of slavery, Georgia has nevertheless included this provision in each of its later Constitutions (1877, 1945).

or hold office who engaged in, or aided in, a duel in Georgia or elsewhere. Others excluded from voting or holding office were idiots and insane persons and those convicted of treason, embezzlement, malfeasance in office, crime punishable by penitentiary sentence, or bribery. At elections liquor was not to be sold, and any voter might be challenged to take an oath that he had not given or accepted any money or treat, and that he had not made any threats.

No significant changes were made in the three departments. The executive department was given a four-year term. The judiciary department was reorganized, the terms of Supreme Court judges becoming twelve years, those of the Superior Court judges eight years. The former inferior courts were abolished. Some shifting of jurisdiction occurred. There was a noticeable enlargement of minute details on the judiciary; it may be that the reason for this lay in the desire to take certain measures out of legislative jurisdiction (as in the case of the social status of the citizen) or to remove certain situations automatically from the power of the judges as they grew in prestige.

An Act of Congress approved June 25, 1868, before admitting Georgia to representation in Congress made a proviso that: "no court or officer shall have, nor shall the General Assembly give, jurisdiction or authority to try or give judgment on or enforce any debt, the consideration of which was a slave or slaves, or the hire thereof." All contracts made during the war for aid of the war were voided, the burden of proof on this point lying on the plaintiff.

Annual meetings of the legislature were to be held. The senate should be elected for four years and the house for two years.

The Constitution of 1865 had provided that citizens could not be compelled to become stockholders in or contribute to a railroad or other internal improvement except in a corporate town or city. Here permission was given to the Assembly to allow the corporate authorities to take stock in such works after an election at which the qualified voters had ratified the proposal. This paved the way for the wave of spending in the approaching era of corporation development. The General Assembly was also authorized upon a two-thirds vote to grant bank charters and suspend special payment, but it was forbidden to pass any laws making the State a stockholder in any corporation, or to lend State aid without one hundred per cent property security. There was a loophole in the clause, "nor to any company in which there is not already an equal amount invested by private persons." Presumably as a protecting phrase there was added, "nor for any other object than a work of public improvement."

The Constitution of 1868 furthered plans for public education. General education was to be free to all children. The office of State school commissioner was created. [20] The revenue derived from the poll-tax, from special taxes on shows and exhibitions and on the sale of liquor, and from commutation for militia service, was set aside for common schools. Furthermore, if these sums should not be sufficient, the Assembly might impose a general tax on property. [21]

The Homestead provision, as finally passed, provided that any head of a family, guardian or trustee should have exemption from execution (except for unpaid taxes, for purchase, money debt, and for debts incurred for improvements, labor and material) on property up to $2,000.00 in homestead and $1,000.00 in personal possessions. A married woman might retain all the property she possessed before marriage, and any

[20] J. R. Little served in this post until 1871; Gustavus J. Orr from then until 1887. In 1866 the University of Georgia was reopened; in 1868 Emory resumed activities. Atlanta University opened for Negroes in 1867, Clark University (started in 1869 as an elementary school) in 1877.

[21] The militia was to consist of all able-bodied males of 18 to 45 years, except as exempt by United States or State Law. No conscientious objector was to be forced to do militia duty; he might pay for exemption.

acquired by her thereafter, free from liability for any debts of her husband.[22]

The Constitution of 1868 was amended only once. The amendment was the result of the administrative abuses following the ratification of the Constitution of 1868, which deserve some attention here.[23]

[22] North and South Carolina were struggling with the same homestead troubles in this Constitution-forming year. Thorpe, *op. cit.*

[23] This was by an act of February 27, 1877, (ratified May 1, 1877) repudiating all bonds endorsed by the State.

# CHAPTER XIV
# RECONSTRUCTION

## I. What Happened to the State

In June, 1868, Congress readmitted Georgia after acceptance of the Fourteenth amendment and the adoption of the two amendments to the Constitution which Congress had stipulated. Members were sent to the House of Representatives but not to the Senate. On July 4 the legislature met. In the house, there was a conservative majority; Democrats one hundred and two, Republicans seventy-three, with twenty-eight Negroes. In the senate, the membership was even, twenty-two members each. From July 4 to July 22 time was consumed on questions of eligibility, but finally on July 22, this matter was settled, the Fourteenth amendment adopted, and Bullock inaugurated. Congress then, on July 28, declared Georgia reconstructed and military rule over. On September 3, the legislators, availing themselves of a technicality in the interpretation of the phraseology of the Constitution, expelled the Negro members, stating that the right to vote does not necessarily mean the right to hold office. Thereupon Congress declared that Georgia had not completed its reconstruction and its Senators were rejected. An anomaly in the situation was apparent when in spite of this, in the November national elections, its votes were counted. Georgia, with Louisiana alone of the Southern States, voted the Democratic ticket and endorsed Seymour and Blair.

In February, 1869, the Fifteenth amendment was proposed. In March, Georgia's representatives to Congress were refused admittance. The matter dragged along, Bullock complaining meanwhile, until, in December, Georgia was required to seat the expelled Negroes and ratify the Fifteenth amendment. In June of that year, in a test case brought before it, the Supreme Court [1] against the dissent of Warner, McKay and Brown con-

---

1 White *v.* Clements, 39 *Ga.* 232.

curring, upheld the constitutional right of a Negro to hold office. Finally, in January, 1870, the Negroes were re-seated and on July 15, reconstruction in Georgia was completed. During this era tremendous public debts piled up, and scandals resulted. Railroad grants were made, the State road was mismanaged, long expensive sessions of the legislature were held. Many towns and cities burdened themselves with debts. Not all the debts, of course, had been incurred in the course of this administration; some of them dated from the period 1865-1868. In 1866 the State issued $3,630,000 in bonds, mostly for the Western and Atlantic railroad. In fairness it might be said that eight hundred and forty miles of railroad were constructed before the panic of 1873 hit the country, and that Georgia was profiting by the money spent by federal soldiers and by the reopening of the cotton market.

Atlanta was quickly becoming the industrial center of the section. Some of its leading citizens—particularly Henry W. Grady, B. H. Hill, J. E. Brown, and A. H. Colquitt—recognized the handwriting on the wall and the inevitability of the industrial era. Atlanta decided to accept Northern capital and the idea of a new South.

Finally, in 1872, the people had a chance at a free election for State officers; James M. Smith was elected governor. In November of that year, Georgia gave its votes to Horace Greeley and the Democrats. In 1874 all provisions in the charters of railroad companies guaranteeing State endorsement were repealed, and by an Act of 1877, the last amendment to the Constitution of 1868, all endorsement of bonds was repudiated.

In the years from 1870 to 1877, there was a good deal of agitation for a new convention to frame a Constitution whose terms would not be dictated by necessity or pressure but by the desire of the people themselves. Other matters, however, were important and pressing and the Convention was slow to materialize.

In 1876 Georgia voted for Tilden. President Hayes, however, came to an agreement with the Georgia Senators, Gordon and Hill, according to which the last of the armies was removed from the State. Then it was, finally, that Georgia could feel itself completely free; it was received again into the union on terms befitting its dignity.

Leadership was resumed in this period by those who had had no share in the work of 1868. For a couple of decades after 1872, Georgia, industrial-minded as it was, accepted the return of the so-called "Bourbons."[2] However, this does not mean that the people were all of one mind. In 1872, there was formed a first granger movement, which was to grow and spread the insurgency of the small farmer groups as it was spreading throughout the rest of the country.

## II. Questions Before The Courts

The varying fortunes of the legislative and executive branches of the government during the reconstruction era have been indicated. Since 1861 it has been written into Georgia Constitutions that legislative acts in violation of the Constitution are illegal and that the judiciary shall so declare them. After the war many new problems, as well as the old accustomed ones, began to make their appearance in the courts. It was the business of the judges to act as a bulwark for the people in this troubled period.

Up to the first of May, 1866, 7,197 pardons had been granted by President Johnson, of which 1,228 were in Georgia.[3] A Federal Court was opened in Savannah on May 9, 1866, so that legal business might proceed. By an Act of Congress of January 24, 1865, it was provided that, before being allowed to practice in a Federal Court, an oath was to be taken by attorneys and counselors should swear that they had taken no part, active or indirect, in the War between the States.

---

[2] Actually until 1902 there was no governor of Georgia who had not been a Confederate leader, military or civil.

[3] Avery, *op. cit.*, p. 360.

RECONSTRUCTION 151

Judge William Law, a man of forty-nine years' experience, applied for admission, and was refused because he could not take the test oath. His case came up as *ex parte* William Law, testing the validity of this act in the District Court of the United States. The act was declared unconstitutional [4] as being a "bill of pains and penalties" with all the attributes of a bill of attainder except death. "If he (the lawyer) keep silence, he is thereby deprived of a constitutional right; if he speaks, he becomes a witness against himself." The act was declared *ex post facto,* in that "an *an ex post facto law* is one which renders an act punishable in a manner in which it was not punishable when it was committed." [5] Ex-Governor Brown attacked the constitutionality of the law creating the test oath. Judge Law was admitted. The Supreme Court of the United States afterwards declared the act to be unconstitutional. [6]

During the period from 1865 to 1872 [7] it becomes apparent that the judges did not reach complete agreement and one finds more and more dissenting opinions. The varying opinions of the judges reflect the indecision of the public.

The cases which came before the Supreme Court in these years cause no surprise. It was inevitable that much concern should be felt for relationships between white and Negro and that tests should be made, for instance, of the right of the Negro to hold office and the validity of debts which involved Negroes as property. In the case of White v. Clements in 1869, [8] the constitutional right of the Negro to hold office was challenged. Two of the judges declared for the constitutionality of the Negro's claim; Judge Warner dissented on the grounds of the last code of Georgia revised after the Constitution of

[4] 35 *Ga.* 285-314, May 1866.

[5] Fletcher *v.* Peck, 6 Cranch 87.

[6] Garland, *ex parte,* 4 Wall. 333 (1867).

[7] Several cases are included up to 1875, based on acts during the reconstruction period.

[8] 39 *Ga.* 232 (1869).

1868, giving the rights of persons of color, in which the political right was not listed. Another instance of divergence were four cases under the so-called "Stay-Law" of 1866 [9] which relieved debtors of their obligations, until January 1870. Chief Justice Warner held that this was an infringement of contract rights. "The obligation of contract is a legal, not a mere moral obligation. It is the law which binds a party to perform his understanding"; "God hath made men upright but they have sought out many inventions." [10] Justice Harris concurred, objecting particularly to the part of the law making it a trespass for an officer to attempt to collect a debt. Justice Walker dissented from the others, stating that he had labored more on this question than on any other submitted to him, because he knew that the will of the people was for it. Nevertheless the majority won and the law was declared unconstitutional.

In the reconstruction period, the judges evidently knew the futility of opposition. In a case that came up in 1867, they expressed their disapproval of an Act of Congress passed in 1862, making certain Treasury notes legal tender. Justice Harris expressed the opinion of the court that the framers of the Constitution had meant money to be hard money, and that Congress had not been given, as an enumerated power, the power to make paper money legal tender. "The Federal Government will become one of unlimited powers," [11] he said; paper money was a war measure, the necessity of which had ceased, and the Act should have been repealed. Then, since he knew he could do nothing about the law, he ended with this rather pathetic face-saver: [12]

> At a future day, should the Constitution be replaced on its ancient pedestal, it may appear that in the decision of this case my action was controlled by laws I could not disobey,

9 37 *Ga.* 124.
10 37 *Ga.* 134 (1867).
11 37 *Ga.* 503 (1867).
12 *Ibid*, p. 507.

RECONSTRUCTION 153

whilst my convictions remained that the legal tender act was an unauthorized exercise of power.

After many years during which it had not appeared at the bar of the Federal Supreme Court, Georgia was again defeated there. In 1867 Governor Jenkins sought to stay the execution of the Reconstruction Acts of Congress by going to Washington to bring suit against the army commanders and the War Department. In the case of Georgia v. Stanton, the Court, "for want of jurisdiction" refused to act.[13]

Judge Lumpkin's death in 1867 had removed the last of the war-time bench. In 1868, Governor Bullock, who became Governor under the new Constitution, appointed a Supreme Court consisting of J. E. Brown, H. K. McKay and H. Warner. With the former two, the judiciary now came into better line with the reconstruction authorities. Frequently Judge Warner dissented.

In December, 1868, the Supreme Court took up its permanent residence in Atlanta.[14] A test[15] on relations between white and Negro arose in a case of marriage between persons of the two races. Leopold Daniels, white, had married Charlotte Scott, Negro, which, according to the code accepted under the new Constitution (1868) was prohibited. The case revolved around the clause that the "social status of citizens shall never be the subject of legislation." The decision was that this status must be left as it always was, therefore the marriage was illegal. It was presumed that each race would be expected to have the same privileges within their own bounds; that is, that Negro churches should be as immune from invasion as white ones,

13 State of Georgia v. Stanton, 6 Wallace 50. State of Georgia v. Grant, 6 Wallace 241.

14 The act of 1906 which established the Court of Appeals made this official. From 1868 on it seems obvious that Atlanta was destined to be the capital though the fight continued until an ordinance attached to the Constitution of 1877 called for a vote between Milledgeville and Atlanta. The choice of the people then definitely located it in Atlanta.

15 39 Ga. 321 (1869).

and that railroads, steamboats and hotels would guarantee to make people of either race comfortable, but not necessarily together. Justice McCay expressed the constitutional point involved as follows:

> Marriage is a civil contract, [its] regulation by law, and I see no reason why the prohibition against persons of different color entering into that contract is regulating the social status of the citizens . . . it may be a good law or a bad law. That is not my affair as a Judge; my only sphere on the subject is to say whether such a law is forbidden by the Constitution. I do not think it is. . . These and such laws have no bearing on the social status of the citizen. They still leave persons to choose their associates, though they provide that they shall not enter into a particular civil contract.[16]

It was not until 1872 [17] (White v. Hart) that a judgment of the Georgia Supreme Court was reviewed by the Supreme Court of the United States:

> The effort of the Supreme Court to reverse the Worcester case in 1832 had been so futile that apparently no Georgia lawyer had, for nearly fifty years, been so bold as to invoke this disputed appellate jurisdiction which had been exercised in hundreds of cases from other States.

In White v. Hart a clause of the Constitution of 1868 was involved, saying:

> No court or officer shall have nor shall the General Assembly give, jurisdiction or authority to try or give judgment on, or enforce any debt, the consideration of which was a slave or slaves, or the hire thereof.[18]

White had a promissory note due March 1, 1860, from Hart. The case had been tried in 1869; Hart, claiming that a slave

16 39 *Ga.* 327-328.
17 39 *Ga.* 306; 13 Wallace 646.
18 Article V, Section 17.

was part of the consideration for the note, had obtained a dismissal. The case was appealed, and the Supreme Court, by a two-to-one decision (Warner dissenting), upheld the decision of the lower court. Warner took the position that this was a valid and legal contract, in which a person had a vested right:

> The emancipation of slaves by war is one thing, the repudiation and confiscation of private contracts between individuals, is another . . . The loss of slave property by emancipation should fall upon him who was the owner of that property at the time emancipation took place . . . This clause of the Constitution of 1868 not only impairs but destroys the obligation of the contract as the same existed under the laws of the State at the time the contract was made.[19]

When the case reached the Federal Supreme Court, it was reversed, Warner's position being upheld. It was in this case that the Georgia Supreme Court was rebuked for saying that the State Constitution of 1868 had been a matter of coercion of Congress.[20] It was also in this case that:

> Chief Justice Chase dissented on the ground that "slavery is against sound morals and natural justice" and pronounced the thirteenth amendment "retroactive." He stood alone. This, so far as I know, is the only promulgation from the bench of a high court of justice of the "higher law" which Seward proclaimed as superior to the Constitution.[21]

The question of the State's power of taxation arises frequently in these years. For example, by an act of March, 1869,[22] a tax was laid on liquor at twenty cents a gallon in quantities less than thirty gallons and a $1,000.00 fine was set for non-payment. The tax money was to be given to common schools, together with a tax on shows and exhibitions. Judge

[19] 39 *Ga.* 308-309.
[20] Robinson, *op. cit.*, p. 610.
[21] *Georgia Historical Quarterly*, VII, Lawton, *op. cit.*, p. 310.
[22] 42 *Ga.* 416 (1871).

McKay and Lochrane upheld the tax and the right of the General Assembly to lay it. Judge Warner dissented. In 1873 a law passed in February of that year, imposing a tax on liquor, was also declared constitutional;[23] and in 1875,[24] in a suit brought by the Atlantic and Gulf Railroad objecting to a tax of one-half of one percent on annual net income as impairing obligation of contract, the tax was upheld by the Court.

In the cases arising over the Relief Act of 1870, providing that one must show he had paid all his taxes before applying to courts to collect debts made before June 1, 1865, Judges Montgomery and McCay concurred in the legitimacy of the Act; Judge Warner dissented, on the grounds that the act was *ex post facto*.[25] He excoriated in no uncertain terms his two associates on the bench "as time-serving judiciary."

An Act was passed in 1869, "to encourage and protect the building of mills and other manufacturing establishments in this State." In compliance with the Act some building was started. When, however, a plaintiff complained[26] that the Conasauga River had been backed upon his land for the erection of a certain mill-dam, the review of the case in the Supreme Court proved in his favor, pointing out that eminent domain may cover only situations where the use is to be for the general public and the owner compensated for damages.

As the newer era of big business approached, and a trend toward monopolies developed throughout the country, a strenuous effort was made on the part of the courts to curb the passing of acts by the legislature which would grant privileges to companies without due protection of property against the right of eminent domain. By an Act of August 1872,[27] the Southwestern Railroad Company was granted a right of way three hundred feet on each side of its tracks, over which it

[23] 49 *Ga.* 195 (1873).
[24] 55 *Ga.* 557 (1875).
[25] 45 *Ga.* 370 (1872).
[26] 45 *Ga.* 501 (1871).
[27] 46 *Ga.* 43 (1872).

RECONSTRUCTION 157

made an agreement to allow the Western Union Telegraph Company to erect telegraph lines. Perhaps partly because of jealousy of an outside company, the Act was challenged by the Southern and Atlantic Telephone Company. The court pronounced it unconstitutional, Judge Warner, in his opinion stating that it failed to provide any process for the enforcing of the payment of just compensation. Said Judge Warner: "The profession of this age requires the frequent exercise of the right of eminent domain, the necessity of right and liberty require that the citizen be paid when he is injured by it, and this court is here to see to it that he is paid."

The stabilization and protection of property and homes after a period of war had been attempted in the Homestead provision of the Constitution of 1868. The eleventh section of an Act of 1868 which had authorized the sale of a homestead violated the Constitution. In a case testing the Act, it was shown that legally this sale could be made only after the dissolution of a family and the consequent cessation of homestead rights. [28]

A check of cases arising under various sections of the Constitution of 1868 will give an idea of their relative importance. Thirty-two cases were based on the Bill of Rights, seventy-eight on the section on the Legislature, forty-two on that of the Executive, twenty-six on that of the Judiciary, and twelve on homestead provisions. The cases cited [29] illustrate not only

---

[28] 55 Ga. 383 (1875).

[29] Some attention was given to the health and welfare of communities. One case occurs [36 Ga. 422 (1867)] in which the situation itself is not so noteworthy as the attention it calls to the conditions of medical care. Two men were trying to recover $107.89 which they had spent in furnishing goods to patients in a smallpox hospital, upon the order of the inferior court of Muscogee County, October-December 1862. An Act of December 1862, had been passed giving the courts the right to make such orders, the funds of which would be furnished by the county, but the judge declared in this case that the Act, though constitutional was not retroactive. The word smallpox always conjures up terror in the people of Georgia, and this case indicates an early effort to segregate it and to provide for the patients. The act itself was constitutional. The two men were given a new trial.

the changing status of the Negro, but the new business interests with their attendant problems. Some of them reflect definitely a sentiment against monopoly, others evince a growing interest in obligation of contract, and protection of property interest.[30] The homestead provision was one of the chief causes of agitation for a new constitutional convention, the main objection to that of 1868 being that it bred irresponsibility on the part of debtors. A study of the reconstruction cases gives a picture of a cross section of Georgia at this time.

[30] Other cases bearing on the interpretation of the Civil War and Reconstruction Constitutions may be found in the following list:

Holt *v.* State 38 Ga. 187.
Jenkins *v.* Mayor and Council of Thomasville, 35 *Ga.* 145.
Vason *v.* City of Augusta, 38 *Ga.* 542.
Black *v.* State, 36 *Ga.* 447.
Comas *v.* Reddish, 35 *Ga.* 236.
Alfred *v.* McKay, 36 *Ga.* 440.
Adams *v.* Adams, 36 *Ga.* 236.
Aycock *v.* Martin, 37 *Ga.* 124.
Cutts *v.* Hardee, 38 *Ga.* 350.
U. S. *v.* Athens Armory, 25 *Ga.* 363.
Smith *v.* Bryan, 34 *Ga.* 53.
Bivins *v.* Bivins, 37 *Ga.* 346.
Wynne *v.* Lumpkin, 35 *Ga.* 208.
Carswell *v.* Macon Mfg. Co., 38 *Ga.* 406.
Martin *et al. v.* State, 38 *Ga.* 296.

## CHAPTER XV
## THE CONVENTION OF 1877

By 1876 the press agitation for a new Constitution was growing rapidly. Many flaws had been found in the Constitution of 1868. Special objections were taken to its homestead provisions; the four-year term of the governor and his appointive power; the location of the seat of government in Atlanta; and the powers of the General Assembly over taxation and bonded indebtedness. As former leaders regained control, they expressed themselves upon the document of 1868. It was, they said, a carpetbag product, dictated for the most part by "negroes and thieves."[1] The only paper in the State opposed to a convention was the *Atlanta Constitution*. The other organs accused Atlanta of fear of losing the capital to Macon—and of disinclination to having the treasury removed to some place where Atlanta could not benefit by its "leaky condition;"[2] The *Constitution* urged postponement of a convention until after the election of 1876. A speech of Robert Toombs in which he roused all the old fears of Negro domination and reconstruction hatreds, probably brought the postponement, so that charges would not be brought against Georgia of Negro disfranchisement and abuse. Some people opposed a convention because of a fear of change; others because the promises to debtors to extend the provisions of homestead exemptions encouraged a tendency to violate contracts. The Republicans objected on principle. On January 14, 1876 the house voted for a convention to be held in 1877. The senate proposed a substitute bill which the house refused, and a conference committee failed. In the summer of 1876 the national election occupied the spotlight, but the issue was not forgotten. A bill passed the house

1 Robert Toombs to the legislature January 1876.

2 Milledgeville *Recorder* quoted in Georgia *Historical Quarterly*, XVII, 192. Atlanta was also accused of wanting to keep the seat of government because the legislators who went to the Assembly spent money freely there on their sprees.

and the senate in January, 1877, after an amendment offered by W. H. Felton,[3] providing for a referendum was accepted.

The referendum came before the voters in June; the voting was light, 48,181 for and 39,057 against.[4] On June 23, Governor Colquitt signed a proclamation for a convention. The place was Atlanta and the date July 11, 1877.

What the people of Georgia wanted and expected from their delegates was well put by the *Savannah Morning News* (quoting the *Lumpkin Independent*) as far back as September 6, 1876. A list of problems for the Convention would include: the saving of money, biennial meetings of the legislature, reduction of judicial circuits, homestead revision, "death and burial of illegally issued Bullock bonds," and unconditional prohibition against State aid to any corporation.

One hundred and ninety-three members, (elected on the basis of population), assembled in the Hall of Representatives of the State capitol on that July day of 1877. Georgia was at last master of its own destiny. It remained to see what lessons it had learned.

Of the leaders who had once held the spotlight, one notices the absence of Joseph E. Brown, in disfavor temporarily because of his stand during reconstruction. Colquitt, the governor, though highly esteemed, was not voted a courtesy invitation to the Convention. His presence might hamper the members' freedom of action. Gordon and Stephens were occupied with national affairs. But conspicuous were B. H. Hill, C. J. Jenkins (unanimously elected President, a sign of gratitude to the old gentleman for his long faithful service) and Robert Toombs, the "unreconstructed rebel", who was to become, as chairman of the committee to revise the constitution, the most active leader of the Convention.[5] It was he who put

---

3 Felton was leader of the Insurgents in the period from 1874-1894.

4 Cited from *Georgia Historical Quarterly*, XVII, p. 203. There were double returns from two counties.

5 Toombs was probably the outstanding delegate on finance and credit, business, the powers of government, and the rights of individuals.

up the guarantee of money to meet the costs of the meeting. Other prominent representatives who figured in committee work and leadership on the floor were less widely known, newer leaders: J. C. Nisbet, W. M. Reese L. J. Gartrell, A. R. Lawton, T. J. Simmons, N. L. Hammond, and Pope Barrow. In his closing speech, Jenkins acknowledged his satisfaction at the presence of friends associated with him of old in public affairs, and his pleasure at observing "many young men who have given unmistakable evidence of high natural endowments and extensive culture. When the responsibility rests on them of conducting the government of this commonwealth . . . they will not be found wanting." [6]

The opening speech of Jenkins was heard with attention. He urged that the Convention avoid extremes, and that it differentiate the fundamental from the statutory law, the general from the local; that it place a barrier against State aid, and provide a limited education for the masses, and higher education for leaders. He would "not caution against class legislation or discrimination," since Georgia was observing strictly its "federal relations." Their work was to devise a government for Georgia within its "reserved sovereignty".

The meeting lasted until August 25. It would seem that no smallest detail of government escaped attention. The reader of the stenographic report may feel that too much time was spent on petty details—that there was, particularly, an obsession about minor expenses and penny-pinching over salaries; but one remembers that these people had been through a very serious economic crisis. Officials had involved them in a heavy debt. While they took care to limit the legislature's control of taxation and grants of credit on State or local faith, they also were careful in small matters.

There was frequent difference of opinion over the powers of the Convention. It was difficult to draw the line between the province of the legislature and that of the fundamental law,

[6] Small, S. W., *A Stenographic Report of the Proceedings of the Constitutional Convention held in Atlanta, Georgia, 1877.*

especially in matters of salary and of election procedure. At the end of seventeen days, some of the convention members started a protest against the waste of time; the most discontented even threatened to take the stump against the Constitution. In spite of the defect of slow progress, the records of the meeting are evidence of the delegates' wide knowledge of parliamentary procedure. They were well-read, thoroughly conversant both with the Constitutions of Georgia and with those of other states, and well posted on finance, corporations, and other current topics. They were also imbued with a knowledge of the wishes of their constituents.

Thirteen standing committees were appointed: Executive, Franchise, Bill of Rights, Judiciary, Legislature, Militia, Finance and Taxation, Public Institutions, Counties, Homestead, Laws of General Operation, Amendments and Miscellaneous, and Education. A Commitee on Revision, headed by Robert Toombs,[7] gave the Constitution its final shape.

Among the major topics under discussion was a provision forbidding the pledging of the State's credit to any individual, company, corporation, or association. Brown, a spokesman for North Georgia, urged State aid for railroads in his district. He asked no wanton use of State funds as in the past, but that convicts or proceeds from their labor be loaned on good security for the building of railroads, turnpikes, or canals. He urged the need of roads through the North Georgia, North Carolina and Tennessee sections. His was an eloquent appeal on economic grounds, on behalf of that part of the State richest in iron, gold, marble, copper, and minerals. The need was urgent to get the corn, wheat, hay and bacon out of the mountains and valleys to market. Apples were selling at twenty cents a bushel which ought to bring two dollars if they could be gotten out, and marble was being imported from Italy and Vermont while beautiful Georgia marble was lying untouched.

[7] The other members were Trammell, Seward, Brown, Gartrell, Mathews, Lawton, William Reese, A. R. Wright.

Robert Toombs, who had come to the Convention primarily to fight the railroads, cited the fact that Pennsylvania with similar experience in overuse of State aid had ruled it out in its latest Constitution and Georgia would do well to do the same. Toombs was probably the man best prepared at the Convention to speak in condemnation of the railroads since he had made this topic under the old Constitution his special study. He said:

> There was not a dollar taken from the treasury under that Constitution that was not a fraud . . . any one of these railroads that ever got its hands into the public treasury was subject of shame and scandal. Nearly all of them broke except the little one between Albany and Thomasville and it will break, too, as soon as its bonds come home.[8]

The original provision against State aid was voted.

The subject of homestead rights came up at least forty times in different forms. There seems to have been no thought of abolishing the homestead provision. The problem was how to retain it (the amount open to debate) and at the same time prevent its being used improperly in order to escape the consequences of debt. At last Toombs took the lead again in saying:

> We have been here about seven weeks and this is the question that has developed the greatest differences of opinion in this house. We have voted both ways upon it several times. . . . Submit it to the people as has been done in New York and other states time and time again.[9]

Finally an Article on Homestead (Article IX) was included in the Constitution, but an ordinance declared that it was not to become a part of the document until after the people had had an opportunity to vote on it. At the next election they would

---

8 Small, *op. cit.*, p. 299.

9 Small, *op. cit.*, p. 428.

be asked to choose between the homestead provision of the Constitution of 1877 and that of the Constitution of 1868.

Another problem was reduction of judicial circuits. The subject of the judiciary came up at least one hundred and four times in various forms. Finally it was decided that regulation of the number of judicial circuits was a legislative function and should not be included in the fundamental law. An ordinance was passed establishing sixteen circuits, until the General Assembly might change them and equalize the labor of the judges in the various circuits.

The act of repudiation of bonded indebtedness by the legislature on February 27, 1877 (ratified as an amendment to the Constitution of 1868 on May 1, 1877), was carefully considered. Jenkins thought that injustice might be done by an unqualified rejection of all such indebtedness. It was decided, however, that this was a matter for the legislature, not for the Constitution.

Certain other subjects which might also better have been left to the legislature were nevertheless imbedded in the organic law: the abolition of whipping and of banishment as punishments for crime, and the prohibition of lobbying. At that very time, according to contemporary reports, lobbyists for the railroad interests were said to be flocking around the doors of the Convention.

A spirited fight ensued from the proposal to pass the following section:

> No bill of attainder, *ex post facto* law, retroactive law, or any law impairing the obligation of contracts, or any law making an irrevocable grant of special privileges and immunities shall be passed.

Robert Toombs again assumed leadership. He desired to force railroads to have their charters replaced by new ones which would take away from them the exemptions from taxation granted in the previous regime. There was, he said, railroad property worth twenty million dollars which had been exempt from taxation for the past forty years. It was time the roads began to be subject to part of the support of the State. Toombs talked for three days about monopolies, perpetuities and spoliation. Jenkins backed him up, making reference to abuses of railroad charters in other states. Other men were against the proposed section. Their spokesman was the same Brown who had urged State support for the back-country roads. [10] Lawson struck the new note in modern industrialism:

> We want mining, banking and railroad companies, and while we ought to guard them so that they may not infringe upon the rights of other people, we should surround them with guarantees that their property invested therein shall not be subject to either legislative caprice or the envy and malice of other corporations.[11]

And Jenkins pointed out:

> I know that a great deal of prejudice has been gotten up against corporations in the public mind . . . Sir, are we at this day to strike a blow at internal improvements? At canals: At manufacturers? No prudent man will invest in any chartered enterprise.[12]

Robert Toombs held out for making it impossible for the State to divest itself irrevocably of any of its powers. He won his point, and the clause he proposed was included, as it stood, in the Bill of Rights. However, it was followed by the stipulation that "no grant of special privilege or immunities shall be revoked except in such manner as to work no injustice to the corporation or creditors of the incorporators."

A long contest took place, as so many times in the past, over the basis of representation in the General Assembly. No more success was achieved than previously. The outcome was the same number of senators from the same number of districts,

---
10 Small, *op. cit.*, 467.
11 Small, *op. cit.*, p. 104.
12 *Ibid*, p. 105.

and the same number of representatives, the only addition being that the representatives of counties were to be apportioned according to population, a revision to be made after each United States census.[13]

Various motives were given for not wishing to combine and reduce the number of senatorial districts to nine as proposed by the committee on revision. One was that candidates would have to travel as much as two hundred and seventy-five miles to canvass for elections. Hill was impatient at this, saying:

> Upon my soul, I know nothing about the wishes of the people upon this subject, but I think that it is safe to say for the people that they want the best government that can be given them for the least money . . . I am sure that with a smaller body, chosen from larger districts than we now have, we would get men who are no more than a hundred miles from home.[14]

Though the meeting had been singularly free from displays of bad temper, recrimination was indulged in at this point. Those who did not want to reduce the size of the Assembly were accused of wanting to insure enough seats for themselves.[15]

Some were in favor of basing the membership in both houses on population. The majority, however, felt that, as in the federal government, distinction should be made between the two houses—that one should represent the counties as sovereignties, the other the population, thus maintaining the system of checks and balances. Robert Toombs insisted that the real desire of the people was for more frequent elections of senators and the retention of annual meetings of the legislature. He fought to secure a biennial election of senators in place of the quadrennial election, and one house at least based on popu-

---

[13] In the various amendments to this section, changes were made in 1904, 1908, 1914, 1918, 1920.
[14] Small, *op. cit.*, p. 347.
[15] *Ibid*, p. 349.

lation. That the meeting of the legislature was changed from annual to biennial was a disappointment to him. He said:[16]

> .... my objection to the present senatorial districts is that they do not represent anything. At least one branch of the General Assembly should represent population, but as at present constituted neither does. I am totally opposed to this system, and I do not favor the one of the committee altogether, but whichever one of them is adopted, I give notice that I shall move that they shall be elected every two years. I want to put power close down to the people, and if I had my way, I would have the legislature meet once every year, and have members of it elected every year. In former times every man went before his constituents every year, and if he was worthy they returned him.

Toombs' theory was that the people are the ultimate source of power.

It is to the Committee on Revision that the successful steering of the work of the Convention should be attributed. Resolutions of thanks were passed to President Jenkins for the manner in which he conducted the meetings, and to Samuel W. Small for his able and impartial reporting of the Convention. The Convention was closed by the President with "well done, good and faithful servant."

[16] Small, *op. cit.*, p. 343.

## CHAPTER XVI
## THE CONSTITUTION OF 1877
### I. Provisions

Under the leadership of Robert Toombs, and with the eyes of their constituents upon them, the gentlemen who framed the Constitution of 1877 tried to meet all needs. Consequently, they ignored the admonition to consider only fundamental law. Many things of a temporary nature were included, and there was certain to be need for amendments as Georgia developed.[1]

On protection of personal and property rights the Convention had been firm. Every care was taken to prevent fraud and monopoly. Irrevocable grants were prohibited. Lotteries were forbidden as they had been in the Constitution of 1868. Lobbying was declared to be a crime. Every male twenty-one years old, resident six months in his county and with all taxes paid, might vote,[2] except that those convicted of treason, embezzlement, malfeasance in office, bribery, larceny or any crime involving moral turpitude, as well as idiots and insane persons, were disfranchised.

Residence requirements for senators and representatives were increased—an evidence of the effort to get rid of "carpet baggers" with short residence, who had been favored in the preceding Constitution.

The power of the legislature to create corporations was limited in that it was not to authorize construction of street

[1] By 1943 the document had become a patchwork. By the time the latest Constitution was proposed in 1945, the amendments had increased to 301.

[2] An amendment of 1908 added: the voter must be a veteran of some war between the Revolution and the War between the States or descended lawfully from one. He must be of good character and understand the duties of citizenship; correctly read in English any paragraph of the Constitution of the United States or of Georgia, or write it when read to him, and be owner of forty acres, in the State, assessed at $500.00. In 1943, the age limit was fixed at eighteen. The provisions of the Constitution of 1945 will be found in Chapter XIX.

passenger railways in any incorporated town or city without the consent of the corporate authorities. The legislative session was cut to forty days,[3] and salaries of members as well as of all officials received more attention [4] in this Constitution than in previous ones.

To be sure that life insurance companies were run without risk to clients, the Constitution provided that both non-resident and resident companies should deposit $100,000 with the comptroller-general. Non-resident companies might show that they had done so in some other state. Fire insurance companies were to deposit with the treasurer whatever "reasonable securities" the General Assembly should enact.

The article on the powers of the General Assembly over taxation deserves a close examination. The sovereign, inalienable right of the people to tax was affirmed. The General Assembly might not make irrevocable grants.[5] Any such former grants were annulled. It was given the power to regulate railroad freights and passenger tariffs, and to prevent unjust discrimination. Robert Toombs was responsible for these paragraphs and for the inclusion of further safeguards against abuse by corporations. The right of eminent domain was not to be abridged, the legislature having the right to take property or franchises from companies as from individuals for public use. By virtue of its police power the State might refuse to allow corporations to conduct business in such a way as to infringe upon the rights of individuals or the well-being of the State. Any amendment of an existing charter or any special law passed for its benefit should constitute a new charter. Com-

---

[3] This has made frequent extensions necessary, the latest being seventy days.

[4] This paved the way for a number of changes as conditions altered living costs. For example, the per diem rate of pay for members of the Assembly was fixed at four dollars. The latest pay is ten dollars a day plus five dollars a day maintenance.

[5] These sections appear to be in line with measures which other states were taking at this same period, while waiting for the Federal government to curb the growing power of "big business".

petition was to be kept free, no rebates or bonuses were to be paid. It was the business of the legislature to activate these regulations. The right to grant corporate privileges and powers was taken from the General Assembly and given to such courts as it might designate. [6]

No vital change was made by this document in the status of the governor. [7] The other executive officers, secretary of state, comptroller and treasurer, were to be elected in the same manner and for the same term as the governor. There is nothing to show that they were not coordinate with him.

In the judiciary department, Supreme Court judges were to be elected by the General Assembly; the system of district courts was discontinued; bondholding judges were disqualified in any bond cases; juries were provided for in all justice courts regardless of the amount in question, and provision was made for the legislature to establish uniformity of procedure for all courts (except city courts) by law.

The Constitution of 1877 devoted an entire article to finance, taxation and public debt. The purposes for which taxes might be levied were specified: for the state government and public institutions; for educational purposes in instructing children in the elementary branches of an English education only; to pay the interest on the public debt, or its principal; for defense in war, to suppress insurrection, or repel invasion; and to supply artificial limbs to soldiers disabled in the Confederate service. All taxation must be uniform on the same class of subjects, *ad valorem* on all property. The General Assembly might tax domestic animals which were destructive of property; it might exempt from taxation public property, places of religious worship or burial, public charitable institutions, buildings for colleges, academies or seminaries, public libraries or other literary

---

[6] In 1891 the Secretary of State was given the right to make grants to banking, insurance, railroad, canal, navigation, express and telegraph companies.

[7] Since that time, by amendment and by the Constitution of 1945, he has been given great power over appointments to newly created boards. See Chapter XIX.

THE CONSTITUTION OF 1877        171

associations, books and philosophical apparatus, public paintings and statuary—if these were not for private or corporate gain. The power to tax corporations should not be surrendered.

Care was taken to list the items for which debts in behalf of the State, or any of its subdivisions might be contracted. Its credit was not to be loaned. Debt in the subdivisions was limited to seven per cent of taxable property. If money were to be borrowed, the purposes must be specified.[8] Counties might levy taxes only for the following purposes: instruction in the elementary branches of an English education; building and repairing public buildings and bridges: maintaining prisoners; paying jurors and coroners; litigation; quarantine; roads and court expenses; and the support of paupers.

The State's property in the Western and Atlantic, Macon and Brunswick, or other railroads and property, was to be sold to pay the bonded indebtedness. Other sections provided for the establishment of a sinking fund; for no donations; and for the letting of public printing to the lowest bidder.[9]

Most of the members of the Convention were much concerned with a system of common schools free to all children, but many exhibited a narrow viewpoint and local bias in their outspoken speeches against anything other than the "rudimentary subjects of an English education."[10] Separate schools were to be provided for white and Negro children. Provisions for the State University were retained, and appropriations were to be made for one State college or university for Negroes. The office of State School Commissioner, appointed by the governor,[11] was kept.

The homestead provisions of the Constitution of 1877 were adopted by vote on the first Wednesday in December. The vote

[8] This section was amended some 124 times.
[9] Probably because of the exorbitant printing bills of the Reconstruction era.
[10] This phrase was dropped in 1912.
[11] This office became elective in 1894. In 1941 the name was changed to that of State School Superintendent.

was 94,722, to 52,000.[12] The amount of property exemption allowed was $1600.

One provision of the Constitution caused more readjustment later than did any other—the section stating flatly that no new county should be created.[13]

Amendment of the Constitution might be proposed by either house. If it passed in each house by a two-thirds vote it was to be published in the newspapers for two months before the next election, when the people were to vote on it.

No convention for changing the document might be held unless each house cast a two-thirds vote in favor of it, and representation in any such convention must be based as nearly as possible on population.[14]

## II. Estimate

It is difficult to estimate the value of the Constitution of 1877. The temper of the membership of the Convention and the tone of the document seem to bear a heavy imprint of Calvinism since there was a great effort to restrain individuals, majorities and government from wrongdoing. In regulating railroads and other corporations, this Constitution followed the general trend of the seventies. Its great length, too, was typical; many state constitutions were being greatly enlarged at this time. Finally, this document goes farther than any previous Georgia Constitution in recognizing the sovereignty of the people.

On September 14, 1877, there was published in Augusta an article entitled *Some Notes on the New Constitution*.[15] The

---

[12] At the same time, it might be added, the Constitution was adopted by 110,442 to 40,947 and Atlanta was selected over Milledgeville by a vote of 99,147 to 55,201. Thorpe, *op. cit.*

[13] In 1904 the number was changed from 137 to 145. Since 1905 sixteen new counties have been added. By merger of certain counties in 1931, the number was reduced to 159.

[14] This feature was never applied, however, since the latest Constitution of Georgia (1945) was devised by commission.

[15] J. Ganahl in *Chronicle and Constitutionalist*.

## THE CONSTITUTION OF 1877

author was obviously interested in business. In spite of that bias, he may be credited with some able criticisms. It appears that Senator Hill had said that any one who opposed the Constitution would "die so fast he won't know what hurt him." The critic said he could wish there had been more investigation and less laudation. He was particularly irked at Robert Toombs, who had damned the Constitution with faint praise in saying that it " would do no harm." To him the chief merits were that the delegates voted down the " wild schemes for equalizing railroad freights which would have driven all through business out of the State." It was a pity, he thought, that such a crusade had been made against the railroads, (indispensable to "all civilized mankind") by those who failed to realize that "the prosperity of the carrier depends on the prosperity of the people." Personal liberty and other personal rights, he said, were secure enough, but property did not receive adequate protection under this Constitution. He did, however, commend the provisions revoking charters, for punishment of fraud, and for reaching the property of debtors concealed from creditors.

Some things, this writer found, were put in odd places, as, for instance, making lobbying a crime. The restriction on the governor's salary, he thought, would reduce the office to a monopoly of the rich, and that on the judges' salaries would not command talent. Finally, he said, taxation and representation were unfairly distributed. Uniformity of taxation was wrong because it is absurd "not to tax a good horse more than a poor one."

So much for the opinion of a contemporary. Looking back from the present point of vantage, it may be said that the Constitution reflected a sincere desire to perfect the fundamental law. That it had to be altered so often was a sign of progress.

# CHAPTER XVII
# AMENDMENTS AND STATUTES 1877-1945
## I. What Interested the People

That the Constitution of 1877 was inadequate to the changing times became increasingly evident in the decade of the nineties. The agrarian revolution had its effects in amendments to the Constitution. In 1890, the legislature was further limited in corporate powers. In 1895, the office of the Supreme Court judge was made elective. The trend of the times, at the turn of the century, is shown by legislation passed about that time enlarging the rights of labor, imposing restrictions upon railroads, and inaugurating fairer election practices.[1] Nevertheless, as in all the other Southern states the Negro was kept out of politics by the "white primary" and by qualifications for voting. A Legislative Reference Department was established in 1914. Interest in the welfare of children found expression in the establishment of a children's court in 1908 and in separate juvenile courts with their own judges in 1915. In 1935, however, a backward step was taken: these courts were closed in all counties of less than 60,000.

In 1931, a reorganization bill was passed to tighten administrative machinery, the educational system and finance. The number of bureaus, departments and institutions was cut from one hundred and two to eighteen.

Between the framing of the Constitution of 1877 and the appointment, in 1943, of a commission to revise it, many changes of importance took place.[2] The General Assembly was given power to grant to the authorities of certain cities zoning and planning rights. By an Act of 1943 equal preference for veterans under civil service was provided. Again in 1943, a

---

[1] Secret ballot 1922.

[2] Governors of the period were: A. H. Colquitt, A. H. Stephens, J. B. Gordon, W. J. Northen, A. O. Bacon, A. D. Candler, J. N. Terrell, Hoke Smith, J. W. Slaton, Hugh Dorsey, T. W. Hardwick, C. Walker, T. Hardeman, R. B. Russell, Eugene Talmadge, E. R. Rivers, and E. Arnall.

## AMENDMENTS AND STATUTES 1877-1945 175

Public Service Commission of five members, chosen by popular vote, was given the power to regulate public utilities.

The governor's term of office was changed from two to four years, and his salary was increased. His power over reprieves and pardons was limited in 1943 to a suspension of execution until the State Board of Pardons and Paroles could hold a hearing. This Board, consisting of three members appointed for seven years, was to communicate in full to the General Assembly the details of each case.

In 1906, a Court of Appeals was created to relieve the pressure upon the Supreme Court of increasing litigation. The Supreme Court, according to a revision of its duties in 1916, was to have no original jurisdiction, but was to hear appeals in the following types of cases: (a) where there was a question as to the construction of the Constitution of the United States or of Georgia, or as to the construction of a treaty, or of a law either of the United States or of Georgia; (b) cases in equity, trials of capital offenses, writs of *habeas corpus,* contests about lands or wills and suits for divorce or alimony. The Court of Appeals was to try cases appealed from other courts in all cases where jurisdiction did not first rest with the Supreme Court. It might certify cases to the Supreme Court for instruction.

A State Highway Patrol Act in 1937 gave Courts of Ordinary the right to try cases where there were not city or county traffic courts.

By various acts passed between 1908 and 1938, counties were given increased powers of home rule; they were enabled to raise taxes for the following additional purposes: sanitation; maintenance of records of births, deaths, disease and health; salaries of county demonstration agents; forest protection; conservation of natural resources; old age assistance; help for the needy blind, and for dependent children; or other welfare purposes.

In 1941, counties and municipal corporations were permitted to contract with each other for such facilities or services as hospitalization. Bonds might be issued for flood protection

(1909), for street improvement (1920), and for hospitals (1929).

The year 1943 brought provision for a teacher retirement system. It also saw a reorganization of the State Board of Education. One member was to be appointed to this Board from each congressional district, the term of office being seven years. Members must be non-partisan, not in the teaching profession, and not connected with any schoolbook concern. Another amendment passed in 1943 defined the Board of Regents of the University System of Georgia. This appointive Board was to be made up of one member from each congressional district and five members from the State at large. The governor was not to be a member of either board.

## II. How the Constitution of 1877 was Invoked

In 1877, the Supreme Court adopted a tone of independence. More laws were declared unconstitutional than at any previous time. In several cases, the charge of unconstitutionality was based on the contention that the rights of the courts had been infringed.[3]

An Act of 1876 requiring any persons engaged in hiring laborers for employment beyond the limits of the State to procure a license at a charge of $100.00, and making it a penal offense to carry on business without the license, was declared constitutional.[4] All people of like business must be taxed alike.[5]

Certain railroad and taxation cases that came up in 1878 seem typical of the period, since protection to the State against irrevocable charters and affirmation of its powers of taxation had been the two major subjects in the Convention. An attempt

---

[3] 59 *Ga.* 60 (1877), 59 *Ga.* 364 (1877), 59 *Ga.* 800 (1877), 60 *Ga.* 138 (1878), 61 *Ga.* 454 (1878). One act had changed the terms of the Supreme Court, one granted courts rights which would violate obligation of contracts to railroads, one conferred power of new trial, one authorized hiring of convicts to private persons for private work, and one changed the provisions for jury trial.

[4] 59 *Ga.* 535 (1877).

[5] 60 *Ga.* 597 (1878).

to tax the Atlantic and Gulf Railroad [6] was challenged on the grounds of violation of contract.[7] The tax act of 1874 was declared constitutional.

The same year (1878) saw a fight over an income tax.[8] Suit against the income tax of the City of Savannah was brought on the uniformity clause. The right to tax incomes, on the ground that income is not property, that "property is a tree, and income the fruit" was declared.

A contest over water rights arose in 1882 between Georgia and the United States.[9] According to the code,[10] any master or commander of a ship must take on board outside Tybee bar the first pilot offering to pilot the vessel across the bar and up the Savannah River. (This did not include vessels sailing between Georgia, South Carolina and Florida). When a company refused to employ a local pilot because of prior arrangements, the pilot sued. He won in the State court under an "implied contract", on the grounds that the Georgia code was not repugnant to the United States Constitution as regards either privileges of citizens of other states or the Fourteenth Amendment. Georgia refused to grant that this was interference with interstate commerce. On reference to the United States Supreme Court, Georgia was overruled.[11]

Prior to the era of prison reform and a "quest for social justice,"[12] the problem of housing and employing usefully of-

[6] 60 *Ga.* 268. This road had been created as a merger out of two older railroads, the Savannah and Albany and the Atlantic and Gulf Railroads.

[7] They based their case on the old Central Railroad and Banking Company case (decided in 92 U. S. 665), a very different situation in which the railroad won its case because there was no intent to create a new corporation. In the present case, the railroad lost since a new corporation had been created, subject to the taxing power of the State.

[8] 60 *Ga.* 93 (1878).

[9] 69 *Ga.* 409 (1882).

[10] See footnote, p. 86.

[11] 118 U. S. 90.

[12] Title of book by H. U. Faulkner, Macmillan Company, New York, 1937.

fenders against the law was a vital one.[13] The State leased its convicts, the labor being regulated by the lessee, but the conditions being under the control of the State as part of its police power, not subject to delegation. In 1876 two companies leased the convicts for twenty years at $25,000 a year.[14] They would in turn let out 250 of these convicts for three-year (and renewable) periods to the Marietta and North Georgia Railroad Company. But by a joint resolution of the Assembly of 1883, the State agreed independently to let to this railroad 250 convicts for three years or until the main line, with its projected branches, was finished. Since no arrangement was made by the resolution for police power, and since violation of contract was entailed, the penitentiary companies sued and won. The act of 1883 was declared unconstitutional.[15]

Between 1892 and 1937 Georgia ran the whole gamut of the prohibition question.[16]

[13] A check of the periodical literature on Georgia discloses that the two questions most frequently discussed seemed to be the convict lease system and prohibition.

[14] 71 *Ga.* 301 (1883).

[15] Following is the history of the lease system: An Act of 1866 arranged for leasing convicts for public works. In 1874 they were leased privately for five years. In 1876 (effective 1879) they were leased to three companies organized by J. E. Brown, J. B. Gordon and W. D. Grant for 20 years for $500,000 payable in twenty annual installments. Medical attention was to be given them, no work to be required on Sundays. They were to be fed and clothed and, when discharged, were to be furnished with a new suit of clothes worth not less than $6.00 and a railroad ticket to their county. In 1887 and again in 1896, the companies were fined for cruelty so that in 1897 the law was amended and the convict leasing system was to be altered when the contracts expired in 1899. A prison commission was to secure a farm where the old, infirm and sick could be housed, the others were to be apportioned, if their term were less than five years, to the counties for chain gang groups; if the term were over five years, they were to be leased, at first at $100 a year, later to the highest bidder. This system prevailed until 1908 when the system was abolished. (Details from Coulter, *op. cit.*, 393-395).

[16] It first tried prohibition of liquor near churches and school houses. In 1885 counties were given local option but this was revoked in 1887. In

An act of 1891 required corporations to give discharged employees or agents written causes of removal, subject to a $5,000.00 fine for non-conformance.[17] The Supreme Court declared the act unconstitutional on the ground that it violated the "right of silence, not less sacred than the right of free speech and writing."

Legislation affecting local educational systems was sometimes contested. Injunction was brought to bear against enforcement of an act of 1883 which charged matriculation fees to students in the city of Gainesville, and extended the school year longer than six months.[18] Of deeper concern, was a case in 1898.[19] By an act of 1872, a county board of education of Richmond, using its discretionary power to establish or discontinue high schools "at such points in the county as the interests and convenience of the people may require," discontinued a school for Negroes. A suit was brought. It was held that, had the school been an elementary school, the Constitution of the State would have been violated, but that there was no such violation in the case of a secondary school.

One cardinal principle was that there should be no discrimination in business. Appeal was often made to the uniformity of taxation clause. For example, the Singer Sewing Machine Company, which did a big business in the South, complained that the general Tax Act of 1886 singled out one business for discriminatory legislation. By this act a tax of $200.00 was laid on each sewing machine dealer in the State, and $10.00 on each of his agents. The tax was held constitutional in that it is per-

---

1907 a prohibition law was passed. Violations were ignored. In 1913 the Webb-Kenyon Act of Congress forbade buying in a wet state and shipping into a dry state. A prohibition act of 1913 allowed each person 2 quarts of whiskey a month, one gallon of wine and 48 quarts of beer, thus being practically ineffective. In 1919 it became a federal offense to make liquor, sell it or possess it. (Details from Coulter, *op. cit.*, pp. 396-399.)

17 94 *Ga.* 732 (1894).
18 96 *Ga.* 477 (1895).
19 103 *Ga.* 641 (1898).

missible to tax all those persons who fall within one general classification.

Discrimination was declared unconstitutional in a case that came up in 1900.[20] The act in question allowed a plaintiff who won a suit against an insurance company to recover attorney's fees as well as damages. This singled out one class, inasmuch as in no other case was provision made for recovery of attorney's fees. Equal protection of person and property was held to be violated.

As early as 1902, one hears of cut-rate drug stores. An association of druggists persuaded the wholesale dealers to boycott an ex-member for cut-rate policies. He sued and won on the ground that this was interference with equal protection of the law, and on the further ground that it was restraint of trade and violated the Anti-Trust Act of 1896.[21]

The United State Supreme Court reversed the Georgia Court in several railroad cases. In 1902, exception was taken to a law which provided that if goods were damaged en route, the railroad company must furnish within thirty days after application a statement as to when, how and where the damage occurred. In one instance,[22] a carload of grapes consigned from Barnesville to Omaha, Nebraska, was damaged. The Central of Georgia Railway, being called upon to furnish a statement as to the circumstances, claimed that the law requiring such a statement was unconstitutional in that it required a defendant to furnish evidence touching the liability of another corporation beyond its own line, and in another state. This, it said, was a violation of the interstate commerce law. The railroad lost its case in the State court, but the United States Supreme Court reversed the decision.

The next year, 1903, saw a similar case.[23] A wholesale liquor dealer in Augusta sent two shipments of whiskey over

[20] Phenix Insurance Co. *v.* Hart (112 *Ga.* 765).
[21] 115 *Ga.* 429 (1902).
[22] 116 *Ga.* 863 (1902) and 196 U. S. 194.
[23] 118 *Ga.* 616 Southern Railway Company *v.* Heymann and 203 U. S. 270.

the Southern Railroad to persons in Charleston, South Carolina. There it was placed in a warehouse of the railroad company where it was seized by constables, and declared contraband: being against the health, morals and safety of the State. The dealer had to refund the purchase price. He sued the railroad company and won. The Georgia Supreme Court reversed the decision and awarded a new trial on the ground that the railroad was not bound to break the law of the State of South Carolina and to resist the authorities of Charleston in the effort to fulfill its contract. The United States Supreme Court again reversed the Georgia court.

Suits in which the United States Supreme Court reversed railroad decisions of the Georgia Supreme Court were sometimes those in which companies tried to escape taxation on the ground of their charters. The reversals (in 1905 and 1906) were based on failure to allow due process of law and on the ground that a charter of a railroad company making its property taxable only in a certain way and to a certain amount can prevent an additional tax on the leasehold of its property. [24]

An Employees Liability Act of 1909 was the basis of a suit in two cases. [25] The railroad claimed that employees who had joined the relief department of the road and accepted from this department benefits for injury were debarred from making further claim against the railroad. The court ruled that suit against the railroad did not constitute violation of the obligation of contract since the government's power to protect people cannot be contracted away.

The United States Supreme Court affirmed the Georgia decision in a suit by the Union Dry Goods Company against the Georgia Public Service Corporation. [26] The defendant had

[24] Georgia Railroad and Banking Company *v.* Wright and Central Georgia Railway Company *v.* Wright, 207 U. S. 127 and 248 U. S. 525.

[25] 136 *Ga.* 639 (1911).

[26] Union Dry Goods Company *v.* The Georgia Public Service Corporation, 142 *Ga.* 841 (1915) and 248 U. S. 372.

made an arrangement with the plaintiff for service at a certain rate. When, by the defendant's order, a higher rate on service went into effect the plaintiff claimed privileges on the basis of its contract. The decision was that the increase of rate was constitutional, being a proper exercise of the police power.

In other cases, freedom of speech was denied in the Georgia court (but upheld on appeal in the Federal Supreme Court); [27] a Workmen's Compensation Act was declared valid; [28] discrimination which forbade Negro barbers to cut white children's hair was declared unconstitutional; [29] and the Housing Authority Act was upheld. [30] The act establishing a Juvenile Court was upheld. [31]

The Framers of the Constitution of 1877 had made it much longer than any previous Georgia Constitution. In doing so, they were probably actuated by two motives—to take out of the hands of the legislature as much power as possible, and to put specific subjects beyond the reach of judicial interpretation. As the years went by and conditions changed, this Constitution proved unsatisfactory and it was further lengthened by amendment. The early years in which it was invoked were times of recovery, shift from agrarian economy to business expansion and an increasing complexity of life, common to the whole country. The work of the Supreme Court became increasingly heavy, since not only the usual tests of criminal, and civil rights were made, but complicated tests of eminent domain, police power, and taxation. After the turn of the century came further tests in which the State's right to enact social legislation was at issue. The judges in Georgia, as elsewhere, had to adjust themselves to the new doctrine of the responsibility of the State for the welfare of its people.

27 184 *Ga.* 613 (1937), 301 U. S. 242.
28 183 *Ga.* 122 (1937).
29 164 *Ga.* 755 (1927).
30 189 *Ga.* 155 (1939).
31 189 *Ga.* 311 (1939).

## CHAPTER XVIII
## GEORGIA FROM 1877 TO 1945

The decade prior to 1877 found many visitors in Georgia. Some had come to view the change left by war; some to observe how Georgia fulfilled its obligations in regard to the reconstruction ordered by Congress; others to invest their money in opportunities offered in rehabilitation, business, and the development of natural resources. They witnessed, in the earlier years, devastation in the sections where war had struck, and poverty throughout, even in those parts which had escaped. A few years later, however, they noticed evidences of progress. Brick houses stood where once were wooden ones, and a grand hotel, the Kimball House, erected in Atlanta in 1870, near the old union depot, was for years the talk of the South, with its silver water cooler, solid mahogany woodwork and stained glass windows.

The seventies saw a real boom in building. The DeGive Opera House, "one of the finest theatres in the South," opened its doors in Atlanta in 1870, and the first street railway (cars drawn by mules) went into operation in 1871. All Georgia hummed with cotton mills. Atlanta fulfilled its potentialities as a great railroad center, and by popular consent the Capitol was built there. On its grounds, as a perpetual link with the past, stood the statue of the war governor, Joseph Brown, with his wife, Elizabeth; inside hung historic flags. [1]

Industrial minded business and professional men, the "Bourbons", led by the triumvirate Brown, Gordon, and Colquitt, exercised control over both business and politics. Mention has already been made of the monopoly obtained by Brown, Gordon and Grant to employ the state convicts in their railroad building and the failure of the courts to uphold a challenge to this monopoly. An independent movement led by William H. Felton tried to wrest control from the "Bourbons" and lent excite-

---

[1] Details from *Georgia a Guide To Its Towns and Countryside*, pp. 165, 173.

ment to politics for years. He "held religious service on Sunday and spoke politics on week-days, and played perilous work generally with personal antecedents." [2] His vocabulary had a "smell of brimstone—few ever came within its wrath who did not get severely blistered." [3] Felton's movement collapsed in 1880 nor could either the Grangers or the Alliancemen stem the tide of business.

In the eighties, the chief spokesman for the new South was the beloved Henry Grady. His statue on Marietta Street in Atlanta stands as a memorial to his leadership. He sponsored local development, manufacturing and diversification of crops. The older statesmen like Toombs and Alexander Stephens had left the stage, and their forensic eloquence was missed in the legislature and on the hustings. But plantation-born Joel Chandler Harris preserved the flavor of the old South in his immortal stories.

The eighties focussed attention on the region in a series of great expositions. An International Cotton Exposition was held in Atlanta in 1881, and a National Exposition in August in 1888. A more ambitious undertaking was the Cotton States and International Exposition of 1895; there Booker T. Washington delivered an address in which he recounted the progress of the Negro.

The newspapers of the nineties were full of talk about housing expansion, and about the growth of business—especially that of the express, telegraph, telephone and electricity companies. Significantly, in 1891 came the first organized labor movement in Atlanta, a movement in line with similar activity growing in the rest of the country since the seventies.

Georgia did not escape the general depression of the nineties, nor was it unaffected by the Populist movement. Tom Watson of Georgia became the spokesman of this movement. After the turn of the century, he was one of the Muckrakers. [4]

2 Avery, *History*, pp. 511-514.
3 Knight, *Bicentennial Memoirs*, I, pp. 85-86.
4 C. Vann Woodward, *Tom Watson, Agrarian Rebel*, p. 376.

In the early part of the new century Hoke Smith, cabinet member in Cleveland's second term, dominated the State scene. He was regarded as the LaFollette of the section. Elected governor in 1906, he increased the railroad commission in size and scope, brought supervision of public utilities, abolished convict leases, and attempted prohibition. The panic of 1907 brought a temporary set-back to reform as did a State constitutional amendment passed in 1908, disfranchising the Negro by registration requirements.

Woodrow Wilson's election in 1912 was hailed with warm pleasure by Georgia, which remembered this Presbyterian minister's son who had hung up his shingle in Atlanta. When, in 1914, the Federal Reserve system was established, one of the district banks was located in Atlanta; the prestige of that city was thereby increased.

The first World War, and the following periods of prosperity and depression, brought to Georgia the same heartache, excitement and anxieties as to other states. In the long road out of depression, more conscious of their responsibility the counties were organized, by the Welfare Department, created in 1919, to administer the Federal and local funds for employment and other relief. The Federal Social Security Act of 1935 crystallized Georgia's thinking on humanitarian needs. The little White House at Warm Springs brought the State into intimate relationship with the New Deal.

In the stretch of time from 1877 to 1945, Georgia, though still cherishing much of the old tradition, moved ahead with the times. The Constitution of 1877 was not adequate. The amendments and statutes which were passed to meet each emerging problem have been previously discussed. The legislature, finally, in 1943, authorized a revision of the Constitution by commission.

## CHAPTER XIX
## THE CONSTITUTIONAL COMMISSION OF 1945 AND ITS WORK

### I. THE COMMISSION

In 1913 came a proposal for a constitutional convention. Of three measures for popular control widely advocated at this time, one, recall, Georgia had already adopted; the other two —initiative and referendum—were still being debated. The movement for constitutional change had, however, no results.[1]

In 1931 the Committee on the Constitution, of the Institute of Public Affairs, held at the University of Georgia, presented *A Proposed Constitution for Georgia* to the round table session. The framework proposed was substantially the same as that of 1877, but it embodied the major changes made by amendment since that time. Again a change of Constitution remained a matter of talk rather than action. It was more and more apparent that the Constitution was not up to date, but not until 1943 did the legislature formally admit the need for a new one. By an act of March 17 of that year it was resolved that since conditions had completely changed since the Constitution of 1877 was framed; since no less than two hundred and sixty-eight amendments—some purely local and temporary—had been adopted; and since inconsistencies had developed as a result of pressure of business in the Assembly, a small commission should be named to draft amendments. These were to be proposed to the Assembly and then with any

[1] The *Bar Association Reports* of that year devoted much space to analysis of the Constitution. The conclusions drawn were: a new Constitution was not needed, it would be better not to change the fundamental law often for fear of making it unstable; the executive should be made more effective in practice as well as on paper; the business of the courts should be expedited; and a graduated income tax was needed. *Georgia Bar Association Reports*, 1913, *Legislative Department*, W. G. Brantley; *Executive Department*, R. L. Smith, *Judicial Department*, Wright Willingham, and *Finance, Taxation and Public Debt*, Walter McElreath; pp. 128-144, 114-127, 145-161, 162-179.

## THE CONSTITUTIONAL COMMISSION OF 1945   187

alterations that might be made, the whole work was to be submitted to the people for ratification. The commission was to consist of the governor, the president of the senate, the speaker of the house, five members of the house appointed by the speaker, three members of the senate appointed by the president, a justice of the Supreme Court named by the Court, a judge of the Court of Appeals named by the Court, the attorney general, the state auditor, two judges of the Superior Court, three practicing attorneys, and three laymen appointed by the governor.[2] It was to report its work to the governor sixty days before the next General Assembly, giving reasons for suggested changes. The governor was to have the proposals printed for the Assembly and published in the press. At the general election of 1945, the people were to vote on the proposals as accepted or altered by the Assembly. It was in this way that the method of changing the Constitution through a convention held for that purpose gave way to a new method—change by commission.[3] Seven sub-committees[4] worked long

[2] The members of the commission were: Ellis Arnall, governor; T. Grady Head, attorney-general, B. E. Thrasher, state auditor; Frank C. Gross, president of the senate; Roy V. Harris, speaker of the house, A. N. Durden, Fred Hand, J. W. Culpepper, Charles L. Gowen, J. Roy McCracken, house members; David S. Atkinson, David J. Arnold, Jeff A. Pope, senate members; Judge Thomas S. Candler and Judge Will R. Smith, of the Superior Courts; James V. Carmichael, Hatton Lovejoy, and Frank Foley, attorneys at law; Mrs. Leonard Haas, R. E. L. Majors and Hamilton Holt, laymen; Judge Warren Grice, Justice of the Supreme Court and Judge Hugh J. MacIntyre of the Court of Appeals.

[3] The Constitution of 1877 had provided for the usual method of change by convention.

[4] Articles I, VI, XII, on the Bill of Rights, Judiciary, Laws of General Operation, and Amendments, were allocated to a committee headed by Warren Grice. Article II on the Franchise and Electorate went to the Committee of which David S. Atkinson was chairman. The two Articles IV and VII on the Power of the General Assembly over Taxation and Finance, Taxation and Public Debt, were worked on by a committee presided over by Hatton Lovejoy, while Article V, the Executive Department, was handled by Fred Hand's committee. Roy V. Harris was chairman of the group revising Article III, with the very difficult task of handling legislative provisions. Sub-committee six, which was headed by Frank C. Gross

and arduously for two years. Finally their work was drawn together and presented to the governor. At the meeting of the legislature in Atlanta in January, 1945, Governor Ellis Arnall presented the document. The attention of other parts of the country was centered on Georgia at this time. Two features of its proposed government called for special notice. Virginia sent a committee to investigate the Penal Board, and Maryland and Tennessee watched the move for Home Rule with particular interest.[5]

As the legislature debated each article, the press aired the question at issue. Comment as a whole was favorable. Only ex-governor Talmadge's paper was in opposition; it maintained that the proposed Constitution was purely an administrative measure—an Arnall idea.

Governor Arnall was advised by the attorney-general that it would be constitutional to submit the commission's document, when accepted or altered by the legislature, as a single amendment.

Day after day the committees on the Constitution in the house and the senate held public hearings. Various groups officially lobbied for their favorite ideas. The county commissioners opposed any county consolidation; the League of Women Voters urged that women serve on juries. It advocated, also, that the state school superintendent be elected by the board rather than by the public. One of the most controversial questions was whether the governor should be eligible to succeed himself. The house committee on the Constitution voted in the negative, twenty-four to twelve. The senate

---

made its proposals on Article VIII, Education, with the understanding that the committee was not in accord on its draft and thought it might be necessary to recommit it for further study. James W. Carmichael as chairman of the committee on Article XI, revising the sections on Counties, turned in a report that the committee was not in accord on means of approval of local laws, whether by the people or by the governing authority. Articles IX and X on Homestead and Militia do not seem to have been assigned to a special committee. Mr. Paul T. McCutchen, Jr., clerk of the house of representatives, served as secretary to the commission.

5 Details from complete file of *Atlanta Constitution* 1945.

committee approved the house vote without discussion. Editorial opinion tended in the same direction; it was thought that the governor would be in a stronger position to advocate the change of Constitution if he were not making it a plank in a political campaign for reelection. [6]

On January 24, the governor, in a speech of an hour and a half, addressed the legislature in a plea for the Constitution. He urged that three measures in particular be included in the organic law: Home Rule, the Merit System and a Prison Board. At last the legislature accepted the report of the commission, and the governor signed it on March 9.

Throughout the summer there was an active campaign led by Governor Arnall for the Constitution.

Besides the governor, the new Constitution had other adherents. De Lacy Allen of Albany, announced candidate for the 1946 gubernatorial campaign, sponsored it. The Georgia League of Women voters and the Georgia Junior Chamber of Commerce were among twenty organizations that supported it. Most of the editors endorsed it. Educators were for it because it made constitutional officers of trustees, county board members and county school superintendents. Veterans were for it because it made special provisions for them. The state treasurer, who was also state director of housing, urged it because it made provision for a state rural housing program. The public had an opportunity to be well posted before August 7, when the vote was taken. On August 5, the *Atlanta Constitution* published a list of fifty of the main provisions of the Constitution. There was little excuse, after the campaign, for ignorance of its contents. The Constitution, as one amendment, was put before the people at the general election of August 7, 1945. Adopted (by a light vote) at that time, it was proclaimed by the governor on August 13. The new "streamlined" [7] Consti-

---

[6] The Constitution as adopted allowed a four year term with no reelection until after a lapse of four years. A move for an amendment to the Constitution to allow Governor Arnall to run again was defeated in a special session of the legislature in January-February 1945.

[7] *Christian Science Monitor*, August 8.

tution of 25,000 words was the second state Constitution to be adopted during the year, that of Missouri being the first.

## II. THE CONSTITUTION

The Bill of Rights was unchanged except for the addition of two provisions, both of which seem out of place: all exemptions from taxation earlier granted in corporate charters were declared null; and ownership of land on tidal water to the low water mark was confirmed.

The article on the elective franchise was brought up to date. Mention of duelling was at last omitted, as was the prohibition of sale of liquor on election day within a two-mile radius of the polls.

The senate was to consist of not over fifty-four members. The size of the house was not specified but the apportionment allotted three representatives to each of the eight largest counties, two to each of the thirty next largest, and one to all the others. This allocation was to be changed after each census. There were not to be more than one hundred and fifty-nine counties.

A new constitutional office was created, that of a lieutenant governor [8] to be elected for the first time at the general election of 1946. Other executive offices specified in the Constitution were attorney-general, state school superintendent, commissioner of agriculture and commissioner of labor. Two new boards were added to the department, a State Board of Correction of five members and a State Department of Veterans' Service of seven members, both appointive.

The Supreme Court was to consist of seven associate justices elected for six years. They were to choose one of their members as Chief Justice and one as presiding justice. The legislature was given authority to add one or more judges of the Superior Court to any judicial circuit or to reduce the number. Judges were given the right to hear in vacation, at chambers, any case

---

[8] Part of the criticism levelled at this Constitution was due to the inclusion of this provision which the people had rejected before.

## THE CONSTITUTIONAL COMMISSION OF 1945

in which a jury trial was not required. The service of women on juries might be required by the General Assembly.

The longest of the articles was the one on finance, taxation and the public debt. New features are that no poll tax was to be levied to exceed one dollar annually upon each poll, and that the General Assembly could exempt from taxation: public property; places of religious worship or burial; charitable institutions; educational institutions open to the general public and their funds (unless invested in real estate); and public libraries. It might also exempt farm products, including baled cotton grown in the State and remaining in the producer's hands for a year.

Exemptions up to $300.00 might be claimed on all personal property except motor vehicles, and there was a homestead exemption to the value of $2,000.00, which the General Assembly might lower to not less than $1,250.00. Property of a value up to $1,600.00 was totally exempt from sale or levy. Provision was made for a rural housing program. Corporations engaging in the rural electrification program were to be exempt until 1961.[9] Common voting stock of a subsidiary corporation not doing business in the State was to be exempt, provided that ninety per cent of its stock was owned in Georgia and that its principal place of business was in the State.

A sinking fund to pay off non-matured bonds was created; pensions might be paid to widows of Confederate soldiers if their marriage had been prior to January 1, 1920, and they had not remarried; construction and maintenance of state buildings and a system of state highways, airports and docks was provided for. Social Security was assured in the taxation program of both State and counties. Other sections had to do with the conservation of the agricultural and industrial resources of the State: public health; fire protection for forest lands; airports; workmen's compensation, and retirement funds. Counties were limited in the amount of debt they might contract, but were

9 As in Act of March 30, 1937, sub-section 1, Section 3.

permitted to accept aid for public construction from the Federal Government, any debt so contracted to be payable within ten years. The maximum debt which the State might incur in order to supply deficiencies was $500,000, the one exception being that this sum might be increased to $3,500,000 if funds were needed for paying public school teachers.

The governor, according to the new Constitution, must submit to the General Assembly, fifteen days after its organization, a General Appropriation Bill.

The article on education contained the notable features of previous amendments: the University System of Georgia; Board of Regents; Board of Education; and State School Superintendent. County boards and independent systems might contract with each other for education, transportation, and the welfare of pupils. Official meetings of boards of education must be open to the public. Counties might levy a tax of not less than five mills and not more than fifteen mills, for educational purposes.

A new article entitled Merit System was added. A nonsalaried state personnel board of three citizens interested in the improvement of public administration, appointed for seven years, [10] was to administer the system. The General Assembly was to provide an actuarially sound retirement system for its employees.

Home Rule for counties and municipalities was provided. Optional plans were to be proposed by the General Assembly. Initiative, referendum, and recall must be included in some of the plans offered for choice.

Watching the returns come in on election night, Governor Ellis Arnall "chalked up another victory over Gene Talmadge." [11] "Georgia," he said, "is on the move."

[10] Except the first, which were to have terms of three, five and seven years respectively.

[11] *Christian Science Monitor,* August 8, 1945.

# CHAPTER XX

## Conclusions

A hundred and sixty-nine years have passed since Georgia's Liberty Boys met at Tondee's Tavern, in Savannah, to plan a revolution. The row of sparsely populated and scattered settlements along the coast has expanded into a great State, dotted with hundreds of cities linked by winding highways.

It is a far cry from the time when the Liberty Boys, the radicals of their day, in legislature turned into convention, framed a Constitution in the midst of the exigencies of war, to the day in 1945 when the youthful Governor Ellis Arnall, a progressive, sometimes dubbed "radical", in the midst of another war, put his name to the Constitution devised by a special commission.

A progressive democracy demands a changing constitution. Between 1777 and 1945, Georgia adopted eight Constitutions in logical succession as the need for each became clear. The brief Constitution of 1777 was designed to care for the immediate needs of a newly independent State which had not yet proved that it could win and maintain its independence. Written in haste and containing only the minimum essentials, its greatest value was in giving a sense of security by a written guarantee of fundamentals. But security was better found in the sword in that day when the seat of government shifted from pillar to post as the tides of battle turned. At times such a state of anarchy existed that observance of a constitutional government was impossible. While in the Constitution emphasis was laid upon the unicameral legislature, the war made it inevitable that the plural executive should assume dictatorial powers.

In 1789, war being over and the weak Confederation having given way to a strong Federal Union, Georgia adopted its second Constitution, patterned closely after the one it had helped devise, in Philadelphia, at the Federal Convention. Conservative in tone, it did not meet the needs of a Westward moving population; this was evident in the effort made in 1795 to revise it.

By 1798 there was a strong movement for changing the Constitution. The Yazoo fraud showed a need to protect the State against abuse by the legislature; other aims were to reorganize the three departments and to satisfy the demands of the more northern sections of the State. The up-country people felt that the existing Constitution did not meet their needs, and they endeavored through various conventions, to secure better representation in the Assembly. These efforts, however, did not succeed; with a few amendments, the Constitution of 1798 operated until the outbreak of the Civil War in 1861. How much longer it would have gone unchanged but by amendment one cannot tell.

The next three Constitutions, those of 1861, 1865, and 1868, were necessitated by the war, its conclusion, and reconstruction. When, finally, the State became again independent, a new Constitution was written which was in force from 1877 to 1945. Three hundred and one amendments were added. Why Georgia preferred to amend rather than change the Constitution is a matter for speculation. Every effort made for a new constitution failed until Governor Arnall made a revision part of his campaign for reform in Georgia.

Since the first two brief Constitutions, of 1777 and 1789, there has been a growing tendency to lengthen the fundamental law to such an extent that it has seemed rather a code of laws than a Constitution. The tendency is a natural one, intimately related to the increasing importance of the common man. With the abolition of property qualifications, the electorate was greatly enlarged. The average man was in a position to exert pressure upon the three departments through election, through the recall, and particularly through the popularly elected constitutional convention. That such pressure was exerted upon the Conventions we have no doubt. They lengthened the Constitution each time, and, by minute detail, fixed and limited the powers and duties of each department and officer. In long articles on taxation, local government, debts, education, procedure, and especially corporations, they exercised a restraining influence. It may have been that they included infinite detail in order to curb the legislature, declaring some things such as the social status of the citizen beyond the realm of legislation. Or it may have been that they wished to clarify issues beyond the shadow of a doubt in cases arising before the judiciary. They gathered together the scattered provisions for rights in the earlier Constitutions, and after 1861 gave them status in a separate article. Here, too, leaving nothing to chance, the most minute and sometimes misplaced details were included.

So far as submission to the people was concerned, all we know in regard to the Constitution of 1777 is that copies were to be distributed. In 1789, when Governor Walton received the new Constitution of that year, he announced it to the town (Savannah) by a discharge of eleven cannon and repaired, with members of the Assembly, to the government house for a glass of wine. The Constitution of 1798 was announced with a sixteen-round fire. But from 1861 to the present, the people have been asked to ratify their Constitutions. In 1945, though the vote on the Constitution was small, a failure to submit it would not have been tolerated.

The principle of separation of powers was advocated but little practiced at first. A check and balance system was nonexistent in the first Constitution. No balance of weight between the three departments was attempted, the one-house legislature having an overweening power, the executive little, and the judiciary practically none. The second Constitution, modeled on the Federal, showed a slight move in the direction of more power for the executive and the judiciary, a move which was extended in 1798, when the legislature was more definitely curbed. Following the adoption of this Constitution came the tendency, mentioned above, to define, by amendment and by new Constitution, specific spheres of activity of the departments.

The framing and operation of the Constitutions of the Civil War and Reconstruction periods form a vital part of Georgia's history, though the Constitutions themselves were necessarily, as things turned out, of a temporary nature, an interlude in the story of the State's development within the Federal Union. In these years, one department grew in importance at the expense of the others. The inclusion, in 1861, for the first time in any Georgia Constitution, of the clause, "legislative acts in violation of the fundamental law are void; and the judiciary shall so declare them," gave the practice of judicial review official recognition.

From 1877 onward, the growing complexity of life has tended to centralize both business and political activity, a tendency which has been reflected in the growing inclination to establish various constitutional boards, thus vesting more and more administrative power in the executive department.

The growth of great business enterprises has brought a tendency, also, to regulate corporations. As was seen in some of the cases reviewed by the Supreme Court, eminent domain was carefully defined; its exercise must be for public use. Corporations have been classified into public, quasi-public, and private. For taxation purposes distinction has been carefully made between those for profit and those for religious, educational and charitable purposes which might be exempt from taxation; between domestic corporations and foreign (in the sense of other states). By statute attempt has been made to control monopoly.

In taxation and finance, the tendency has been to make the law uniform, general and for public purposes only; to fix a maximum rate and a maximum debt.

In these movements Georgia has not been alone. The trends have appeared to be more or less uniform, varying only in detail, throughout the country. In some respects Georgia has taken the lead. The movement in 1945 for increased Home Rule was watched with interest by other states; so too, were

# CONCLUSIONS

the Merit system, for the selection of State personnel, and the abolition of the poll tax as an electoral qualification.

Quite in keeping with the purposes for which Georgia was founded, there has been evident an increasing social consciousness. A humanitarian motive prompted the establishment of the Colony of Georgia. The early Constitutions made no provision for welfare, but early State legislation authorized the formation of societies, lodges and other semi-social charitable institutions. As counties and cities more and more provided for the unfortunate through local welfare agencies, interest was created in social security; when the Federal Social Security Act of 1935 was passed the ground was already prepared. The Constitution of 1945 embodies the principles of this act. Through its home rule provisions, it also makes it possible for sub-divisions of the State to inaugurate programs of rural housing, electrification, and hospitalization.

How long the Constitution of 1945, in its present form, will serve the needs of the State is a matter of conjecture. It may be that dynamic Georgia will need further changes in its Constitution.

# BIBLIOGRAPHY

PRIMARY SOURCES

*Acts and Resolutions of the General Assembly of the State of Georgia, 1821-1855*, Milledgeville; 1869-1873, 1875-1935, Atlanta; 1874, Savannah.
*Annual Reports and Opinions of the Attorney General's Office.* Atlanta, J. P. Harrison Company, 1904.
Bartram, William, *The Travels of William Bartram.* Mark Van Doren, ed., Macy-Masius, 1928.
Catterall, H. T., ed., *Judicial Cases Concerning American Slavery and the Negro*, 5 vols. Washington, Carnegie Institute, 1932.
Charlton, R. M., *Reports of Decisions Made in the Superior Court of the Eastern District of Georgia, 1811-1837.* Savannah, T. Purse Company, 1838.
Charlton, T. U. P., *Reports of Cases Argued and Determined in the Superior Courts of the Eastern Circuit of Georgia, 1805-1810.* Utica, New York, S. Gould and Son, 1824.
*The Colonial Records of the State of Georgia.* Compiled and published by Allen D. Candler, Atlanta, 1904-1915.
Commager, H. S., *Documents of American History.* New York, F. S. Crofts Company, 1943.
*The Confederate Records of the State of Georgia.* Compiled and published by Allen D. Candler, Atlanta, 1909-1911.
*Compilation of the Laws of the State of Georgia:*
   1800-1810, Clayton, A. S., Augusta, Adams and Duychanicks, 1812.
   1810-1819, Lamar, L. Q. C., Augusta, T. S. Harmon, 1821.
   1819-1829, Dawson, W. C., Milledgeville, Grantland and Orme, 1831.
*Constitutions of the State of Georgia:*
   (1) 1777, 1789, 1798 and amendments of 1795 in *Digest of Laws of State of Georgia*, H. Marbury and W. H. Crawford, Louisville, Seymour Woolhopter Stebbins, 1802.
   (2) All Constitutions 1777, 1789, 1798, 1861, 1865, 1868, 1877, in McElreath, Walter, *A Treatise on the Constitution of Georgia.* Atlanta, J. P. Harrison Company, 1912.
   (3) Constitution of the State of Georgia—Ratified, the 6th of May, 1789. Printed by John E. Smith, Printer to the State, MDCCLXXIX.
   (4) Constitution of the State of Georgia. A. M. Millan, Printer to the State, MDCCXCVIII.
   (5) Constitution of the State of Georgia as adopted by General Assembly, session of 1945, ratified by the people, August 7, 1945, and proclaimed by the governor August 13, 1945.
*Cursory Remarks on Men and Measures in Georgia.* A Citizen, Savannah, 1784.
Davidson, Grace Gillam, *Early Records of Georgia—Wilkes County*, 2 vols. Macon, J. W. Burke Company, 1932.

De Bow, J. D. B., *Industrial Resources of the Southern and Western States.* New Orleans, Office of De Bow's Review, 1852.

Digests of Statutes and Laws:

Clark, R. H., Cobb, T. R. R., Irwin, D., *Code of the State of Georgia.* Atlanta, John H. Sears, 1861. Atlanta, Franklin Steam Printing House, 1867.

Cobb, Howell, *Analysis of Statutes of Georgia.* New York, E. O. Jenkins, 1846.

Cobb, T. R. R., *Digest of Laws of State of Georgia Prior to 1851.* Athens, Christy, Kelsea and Beuhe, 1851.

Marbury, H. and Crawford, W. H., *Digest of the Laws of the State of Georgia.* Louisville, Seymour, Woodhopter, Stebbins, 1802.

Prince, O. H., *Digest of the Laws of Georgia.* Milledgeville, Grantland & Orme, 1822.

Schley, W., *Digest of English Statutes of Force in the State of Georgia on May 14, 1776.* Philadelphia, J. Maxwell, 1826.

Downing, Hugh U., *Cases in Georgia Reports and Georgia Court of Appeals Reports that have been overruled, doubted, criticized or modified.* Compiled by Hugh U. Downing of the Columbus Bar, 1922.

Dudley, G. M., *Reports of Decisions Made by Judges of Superior Courts of Law and Chancery of the State of Georgia, 1821-1833.* New York, Collins Keese Company, 1837.

Elliot, Jonathan, *The Debates in the Several State Conventions on the Adoption of the Federal Constitution.* 5 vols. Philadelphia, Lippincott, 1836-1845.

Felton, R. L., *My Memoirs of Georgia Politics.* Atlanta, Index Printing Company, 1911.

Harper, R. G., *The Case of the Georgia Sales on the Mississippi Considered.* Philadelphia, Richard Folwell, 1799.

*Journal of the Conventions of 1789, 1795, 1798,* (Manuscript). Archives Atlanta, Georgia.

*Journal of the Convention of the State of Georgia,* Louisville, 1795. Augusta, McMillan, 1795.

*Journal of the General Convention of the State of Georgia to Reduce the Members of the General Assembly.* Milledgeville, Federal Union Office, 1833.

*Journal of the Convention to Reduce and Equalize the Representation of the General Assembly of the State.* Milledgeville, P. L. Robinson, 1839.

*Journal of the State Convention held in Milledgeville, December, 1850.* Milledgeville, R. M. Orme, 1850.

*Journal of the Public and Secret Proceedings of the Convention of the People of Georgia.* Milledgeville, Houghton, Nisbet & Barnes, 1861.

*Journal of the Proceedings of the Convention of the People of Georgia, Milledgeville, 1865.* Milledgeville, R. M. Orme, 1865.

*Journal of the Proceedings of the Constitutional Convention, 1867-1868.* Augusta, E. K. Pughe, 1868.

## BIBLIOGRAPHY

*Journal of the Constitutional Convention of the People of Georgia.* Atlanta, J. P. Harrison Company, 1877.
Leigh, F. B., *Ten Years on a Georgia Plantation Since the War.* London, Bentley, 1883.
McCafferty, J. M., *Decisions of the Superior Courts of the State of Georgia, 1842-1843,* 2 vols. Augusta, 1843-1844.
Park, O. A., *Code of Georgia Annotated.* Atlanta, Harrison Co., 1935—
———. *Digest of Decisions of Supreme Court and Court of Appeals of Georgia on Banks and Banking.*
*Proceedings of the Georgia Conference on Social Work.* Tenth annual meeting, Columbus, April 14-17, 1935.
*Proceedings of the Freedmen's Convention.* Augusta, 1866.
*Proceedings of the Georgia Equal Rights Association.* New York, April 4, 1866.
*Reports of Cases Decided in the Court of Appeals of the State of Georgia, January and March Terms, 1907-1945,* vols. 1-72. Atlanta, J. P. Harrison Co., 1907-1945.
*Reports of Cases Decided in the Supreme Court of the State of Georgia,* vols. 1-199. 1847-1945.
*The Revolutionary Records of the State of Georgia.* Compiled and Published by Allen D. Candler, Atlanta, 1908.
*Stenographic Report of Proceedings of the Constitutional Convention of 1877,* S. W. Small.
*United States Reports—Cases Argued and Adjudged in the Supreme Court.*
Wilson, Caroline Price, *Annals of Georgia—Liberty County Records and a State Revolutionary Payroll,* vol. I. New York, The Grafton Press, 1928.
Wylie, Lollie Belle, *Memoirs of Judge Richard H. Clark.* Atlanta, Franklin Printing and Publishing Company, 1898.
Thorpe, F. N., *The Federal and State Constitutions,* 7 vols. Washington, Government Printing Office, 1909.

### SECONDARY SOURCES

*General*

*Appleton's Cyclopaedia of American Biography.* Ed. by J. G. Wilson and John Fiske, New York, D. Appleton and Company, 1900.
Aumann, F. R., *The Changing American Legal System.* Columbus, Ohio University Press, 1940.
Beard, C. A., *The Supreme Court and the Constitution.* New York, Paisley Press, 1938.
Boudin, L. B., *Government by Judiciary.* New York, W. Godwin Company, 1932.
Bryce, James, *The American Commonwealth.* New York, The Macmillan Company, 1896, 1906.
Carr, R. K., *The Supreme Court and Judicial Review.* New York, Farrar and Rhinehart, 1942.

Channing, E., *History of the United States,* 6 vols. New York, The Macmillan Company, 1912-1926.
Commager, H. S., *Majority Rule and Minority Rights.* New York, Oxford University Press, 1943.
Corwin, E. S., *Doctrine of Judicial Review.* Princeton, Princeton University Press, 1914.
*Dictionary of American Biography,* D. Malone, ed. New York, Scribner's, 1928-1944.
Dodd, W. F., *State Government.* New York, The Century Company, 1924, 1928.
Dunning, W. A., *Essays on Civil War and Reconstruction.* New York, The Macmillan Company, 1904.
Faust, A. B., *The German Element in the United States.* New York, Houghton, Mifflin Company, 1909.
Greene, E. B., *Foundations of American Nationality.* New York, American Book Company, 1922.
Haines, C. G., *The American Doctrine of Judicial Supremacy.* Berkeley, University of California Press, 1932.
Hicks, John D., *The Populist Revolt.* Minneapolis, The University of Minnesota Press, 1931.
Hildreth, Richard, *The History of the United States of America,* 6 vols. New York, Harper Brothers, 1877-1880.
Kettleborough, Charles, *Constitution Making in Indiana.* Indianapolis, Indiana Historical Collections, 1916-1930.
McIlwain, *Constitutionalism and the Changing World.* New York, The Macmillan Company, 1939.
McClure, Wallace, *State Constitution Making—With Especial Reference to Tennessee.* Nashville, Marshall and Bruce, 1916.
Merriam, C. E., *A History of American Political Theories.* New York, The Macmillan Company, 1918.
Moore, A. B., *Conscription and Conflict in the Confederacy.* New York, The Macmillan Company, 1924.
Nevins, A., *The American States During and After the Revolution.* New York, The Macmillan Company, 1924.
Osgood, H. L., *American Colonies in the Eighteenth Century,* 4 vols. New York, Columbia University Press, 1929.
Robinson, W. M. Jr., *Justice in Grey.* Cambridge, Harvard University Press, 1941.
Schlesinger, A. M., *The Colonial Merchants and the American Revolution.* New York, Facsimile Library Inc., 1939.
Stephens, A. H., *Constitutional View of the Late War Between the States.* Philadelphia, Zeigler, McCurdy Company, 1868-1870.
Thorpe, F. N., *Constitutional History of the United States,* 3 vols. Chicago, Callaghan and Company, 1901.
Warren, C., *History of the Harvard Law School,* 2 vols. New York, Lewis Publishing Company, 1908.

———. *The Supreme Court in United States History*, 2 vols. Boston, Little Brown Company, 1935.
Wilson, W., *Constitutional Government in the United States.* New York, Columbia University Press, 1908.
Wright, B. F., *The Growth of American Constitutional Law.* New York, Houghton, Mifflin Company, 1942.

## Georgia

Avery, I. W., *In Memory. The Last Sickness, Death and Funeral Obsequies of Alexander H. Stephens.* Atlanta, V. P. Sisson, Publisher, 1883.
———. *The History of the State of Georgia from 1850 to 1881.* New York, Brown and Derby, 1881.
Arnett, A. M., *The Populist Movement in Georgia.* New York, Columbia University Press, 1926.
Barrow, Elfrida De Renne and Bell, Laura Palmer, *Anchored Yesterdays.* Savannah, Review Publishing and Printing Company, 1923.
Beeson, Leola S., *History Stories of Milledgeville and Baldwin County.* Macon, the J. W. Burke Company, 1943.
Bland, J. M., *Georgia and the Federal Constitution.* Washington, U. S. Government Printing Office, 1937.
Bonner, J. C., and Roberts, L. E., *Studies in Georgia History and Government.* Athens, University of Georgia Press, 1940.
Brooks, R. P., *The Agrarian Revolution in Georgia.* Madison, The University of Wisconsin Press, 1914.
Charlton, T. U. P., *Life of Major General J. Jackson.* Augusta, G. F. Randolph Company, 1805.
Cleveland, Henry, *Alexander H. Stephens.* Philadelphia, National Publishing Company, 1866.
Coulter, E. M., *A Short History of Georgia.* Chapel Hill, University of North Carolina Press, 1933.
Evans, L. B., *All About Georgia—Two Hundred Years of Romance and Reality.* New York, American Book Company, 1933.
———. *History of Georgia.* N. Y. Universal Publishing Company, 1903.
Flippin, P. S., *Herschel V. Johnson of Georgia, State Rights Unionist.* Richmond, Virginia, Dietz Printing Company, 1931.
Gamble, Thomas, *Savannah Duels and Duellists, 1733-1877.* Savannah, Review Publishing and Printing Company, 1932.
*Georgia A Guide to Its Towns and Countryside.* Compiled and written by workers of the Writers Program of the Works Progress Administration, Athens, University of Georgia Press, 1940.
Gilmer, George R., *Sketches of Some of First Settlers of Upper Georgia* (Reprint of Gilmer's *Georgians*). Georgia, Americus Book Company, 1926.
Gosnell, C. B., *Government and Politics of Georgia.* New York, T. Nelson Sons, 1936.

Harden, William, *A History of Savannah and South Georgia*, vol. 1. Chicago, The Lewis Publishing Company, 1913.
Howell, C., *History of Georgia*, 4 vols. Atlanta, S. J. Clarke, 1926.
Institute of Public Affairs: *Hearings on Judicial Revision Before Senate Committee on Judicial and Legislative Reform*. Athens, University of Georgia, 1932.
Jenkins, Charles Francis, *Button Gwinnett—Signer of the Declaration of Independence*. New York, Doubleday, Page and Company, 1926.
Johnson, Amanda, *Georgia as Colony and State*. Atlanta, W. W. Brown Company, 1938.
Johnston, R. M. and Browne, W. H., *Life of Alexander H. Stephens*. Philadelphia, Lippincott and Company, 1878.
Jones, C. C., *History of Georgia*, 2 vols. Boston, Houghton, Mifflin Company, 1883.
——. *History of Savannah, Georgia, from Its Settlement to the Close of the Eighteenth Century*. Syracuse, D. Mason and Company, 1890.
——. *Midway Church Address*. August, 1889.
——. *The Dead Towns of Georgia*. Savannah, Morning News Steam Printing House, 1878.
——. *Biographical Sketches of the Delegates from Georgia to the Continental Congress*. New York, Houghton, Mifflin, 1891.
Knight, L. L., *Bicentennial Memoirs and Memories*. Atlanta, Published by author for private distribution, 1933.
——. *Encyclopedia of Georgia Biography*. Atlanta, A. H. Carston, 1931.
——. *Georgia Landmarks, Memorials and Legends*. Atlanta, Byrd, 1913-1914.
McCain, J. R., *The Executive in Proprietary Georgia*. Atlanta, 1914.
——. *Georgia as a Proprietary Province*. Boston, R. G. Badger, 1917.
McCall, H., *History of Georgia Up to Present Day*, 2 vols. Savannah, Seymour and Williams, 1811-1816.
McElreath, Walter, *A Treatise on the Constitution of Georgia*. Atlanta, Harrison Company, 1912.
Miller, S. F., *Bench and Bar of Georgia*, 2 vols. Philadelphia, J. B. Lippincott, 1858.
Northen, W. J., *Men of Mark in Georgia*, 6 vols. Atlanta, A. B. Caldwell, 1907-1912.
Phillips, U. B., *Georgia and State Rights*. Washington, Government Printing Office, 1902.
——. *The Life of Robert Toombs*. New York, The Macmillan Company, 1913.
Reed, John C., *The Brothers' War*. Boston, Little, Brown and Company, 1905.
Saye, Albert B., *New Viewpoints in Georgia History*. Athens, University of Georgia Press, 1943.
Sherwood, Abiel, *A Gazetteer of the State of Georgia*. Athens, University of Georgia Press, 1939. Reprinted from original published in 1827.

Shryock, R. H., *Georgia and The Union in 1850*. Philadelphia, University of Pennsylvania, 1926.
Smith, George Gillman, *The Story of Georgia and the Georgia People—1732-1860*. Macon, G. G. Smith Publishing Company, 1900.
Stevens, W. B., *History of Georgia*, 2 vols. Philadelphia, E. H. Butler Company, 1859.
White, George, Rev., *Historical Collections of Georgia*. New York, Pudney and Russell, 1855.
——. *Statistics of the State of Georgia*. Savannah, W. Thorne Williams, 1849.
Woolley, E. C., *Reconstruction of Georgia*. New York, Columbia University Press, 1901.
Strickland, R. C., *Religion and the State in Georgia in the Eighteenth Century*. New York, Columbia University Press, 1939.
Thompson, C. M., *Reconstruction in Georgia, Economic, Social, Political, 1866-1872*. Columbia University Studies in History, Economics and Public Law LXIV, 1915.
Wilson, Adelaide, *Historic and Picturesque Savannah*. Published by the Subscribers, Boston Photogravure Company, 1889.
Woodward, C. Vann, *Tom Watson, Agrarian Rebel*. New York, The Macmillan Company, 1938.

*Articles*

*Annals of the American Academy of Political and Social Science*. Callender, C. H., ed.
  *The State Constitution of the Future*. 1935.
  *Our State Constitutions*. Dealy, James Q., 1907.
*Annual Reports of the American Historical Association*, 1911, vol. 2. *The Correspondence of Robert Toombs, Alexander H. Stephens and Howell Cobb* (Edited by U. B. Phillips).
*Encyclopedia of the Social Sciences*. Seligman, R. A., ed. New York, The Macmillan Company.
*Georgia Historical Quarterly*. Savannah, Georgia Historical Society, 1917-.
*Georgia Lawyer*, vol. 1-2, 1930-1932. Macon, Georgia Lawyer Publishing Company, 1930-1932.
*Journal of Southern History Quarterly*. Southern Historical Association, 1935-.
*Publications of the Southern History Association*. Washington, D. C., 1897-.
*Reports of the Proceedings of the Annual Conventions of the Georgia Bar Association*, 1885-. Macon and Atlanta, 1888-1942.
*Southern Historical Society Papers*. Richmond, Virginia, 1876-1943.
*Southern Quarterly Review*. Charleston, South Carolina, 1840-.

OTHER SOURCES

*Newspapers*

Atlanta *Constitution*, 1868, 1877, 1885, 1886, 1890, 1891, 1893, 1900, 1921-1931, 1938, 1945.

Atlanta *Daily Intelligencer*, 1868.
Atlanta *Daily New Era*, 1867, 1868.
Augusta *Chronicle and Constitutionalist*, September 14, 1877. Ganahl, J., *Notes on the New Constitution*.
Augusta *Daily Chronicle* and *Sentinel*, 1861, 1865, 1885, 1887.
Augusta *Daily Constitutionalist*, 1861, 1865, 1867, 1868.
*Christian Science Monitor*, 1926, 1935, 1945.
*Georgia State Gazette*, 1789.
*Griffin Tri-Weekly Star*, 1868.
New York: *Herald, Post, Sun, Times, World* (items in New York Historical Society Collection and clippings bureau of Columbia Journalism Library).
Philadelphia: *Daily Evening Telegraph* (scattered).
    *Press*, 1890.
Savannah: *Columbian Museum* and *Savannah Advertiser*, 1798.
    *Daily Herald*, 1865.
    *Daily Times*, 1891.
    *Morning News*, 1861, 1890.
    *National Republican*, 1865.
    *World*, 1887.

# INDEX

Admisson to bar, 44-45 n, 72
Agrarian Revolution, 174
Alleviating Acts, 94
Alterations, 46, 70, 90
Amicable Society, 16
Andrew, Benjamin, 17 n, 13
Anglican Church, 13
Arnall, Ellis, 187 n, 188, 189, 192
Articles of Confederation, 32, 56
Assembly, 11, 20, 29, 40, 41, 42 n, 68, 80
Atlanta, 111, 139, 153 n, 183
Atlanta Law School, 72 n
Augusta, 11, 13, 24 n, 45 n, 50, 52, 58, 73, 94, 95, 104, 106, 127

Baldwin, Abraham, 33 n, 54, 55, 56, 58, 87 n
Bank of U. S. v. Deveaux, 72 n
Bartram, William, 17 n
Benefit of Clergy, 92 n
Berrien, J. M., 87 n, 94, 96 n, 109, 110
Bill of rights, 34, 47, 65, 80
Bissell, Alexander, 51
Blackstone, 101
Board of Correction, 190
Board of Pardons and Paroles, 175
Bonds, 149, 164, 191
Boston Port Bill, 19
Boston Tea Party, 18
Bourbons, 150, 183
Brown, J. E., 112, 114, 117, 124, 130, 135, 149, 153, 160, 183
Brownson, Nathan, 13, 41 n, 62 n, 64 n
Bullock, Archibald, 19, 21, 22, 24, 26, 31, 33 n, 56
Bullock, R. B., 136, 142, 144, 148

Charlton, T. U. P., 94, 107
Cherokee Nation v. Georgia, 71 n
Chief Justice, 42, 44, 98
Chisholm v. Georgia, 71, 104 n
Clarke, John, 108
Cobb, Howell, 112, 114, 118, 119
Cobb, T. R. R., 112, 114, 117, 118, 120
Code, 86 n, 93, 101 n
Codes, 13
Colquitt, A. H., 87 n, 114, 117, 149
Committees of Correspondence, 47
Commons House, 15
Compilations, 86 n
Conclusions, 193-197

Confederacy, 125
Confederate Constitution, 119
Congregationalists, 12
Conscription, 124
Constitution, Confederate States, 72 n
Constitution, first, 25-26
Constitution, 1777, 30, 32, 34, 53
Constitution, 1789, 65-70
Constitution, 1798, 37 n, 73 n, 79-90, 91-106, 107
Constitution, 1861, 122-124
Constitution, 1865, 123 n, 132-134
Constitution, 1868, 123 n, 144-147
Constitution, 1877, 124 n, 144 n, 168-173
Constitution, 1945, 124 n, 144 n, 168 n, 190-192
Constitutional Commission, 1945, 186-190
Constitutionality, 53, 91, 98, 101
Constitutional principles, 20
Constitutional rights, 14, 18, 19, 21
Constitutional Union Party, 110
Continental Congress, 20, 22, 24, 26, 29, 31, 32, 37, 75
Contract, 105
Convention, Ratification Federal Constitution, 59
Convention, 1788, 62
Convention, 1789, 63-64, 77
Convention, 1795, 31, 75, 77
Convention, 1798, 31, 77
Convention, 1861, 114-121
Convention, 1865, 115 n, 127-132
Convention, 1867-1868, 135-144
Convention, 1887, 159-167
Convicts, 178 n
Cooper v. Telfair, 35 n
Corporations, 146
Council, 12, 20, 36, 38, 40, 41, 49
Council of Safety, 22
Counties, 36, 45, 172, 190, 191
Court-merchant, 44, 69, 84
Court of Appeals, 23 n, 99 n, 175
Courts of Chancery, 23 n
Courts of Conscience, 23 n, 44, 69
Crackers, 14
Crawford, G. W., 114, 120
Crawford, W. H., 94, 107, 108, 109

## INDEX

Darien, 11, 13, 104
Davis, Jefferson, 118 n, 119
Debtors, 88
Debts, 171
Declaration of Independence, 24, 26, 29, 31, 34, 47, 52, 122
Delegation of power, 99, 102, 106
Digest, 34 n, 53, 79, 86 n, 104 n
Discrimination, 180, 182
Divorces, 73, 80, 86
Dorchester, 12, 17 n
Drayton, William Henry, 32-33
Dred Scott Case, 104 n
Duelling, 144, 190
Due Process, 181

Ebenezer, 24 n, 32, 49
Education, 13, 45, 54, 90 n, 133, 146, 171, 176, 192
Election, 1860, 111
Eleventh amendment, 71
Eminent domain, 99, 101 n, 156, 169, 182
Emory University, 72 n
Equal protection, 180
Estates, 38 n, 70, 73
Executive, Constitution 1777, 39
Executive, Constitution 1789, 68
Executive, Constitution 1798, 84
Exemptions, 96
*Ex parte* William Law, 151
*Ex post facto*, 19, 88, 95, 156

Federal Constitution, 119
Federal Convention, 31 n, 55 n, 57-58
Federal Courts, 106
Federalists, 107
Federal Supreme Court, 101, 106
Felton, W. H., 160, 183
Few, William, 30, 31, 33 n, 45 n, 50, 56, 57 n, 58, 62 n
Fifteenth Amendment, 148
Fletcher v. Peck, 71, 74 n
Forsyth, John, 109
Fourteenth Amendment, 132, 135, 139, 148
Freedmen, 131
Freedom of speech, 182
Free Negroes, 89 n, 97, 99, 104
Free persons of color, 133

General Appropriation Bill, 192
General Assembly, 120
General gaol delivery, 23 n
*Georgia Gazette*, 12, 18, 60, 64
Georgia Medical Society, 75 n
Georgia v. Stanton, 153 n

Gibbons, William, 63, 64 n
Gibbons v. Ogden, 111
Glen, John, 19, 20, 33, 42 n, 43 n
Governor Wright, 12, 15, 16, 19, 22, 23, 24
Grady, Henry W., 149, 184
Great Seal, 45, 84
Green bag, 92 n
Gwinnett, Button, 13, 24, 30, 31, 32, 33, 56

*Habeas Corpus*, 32, 46, 70, 88, 92 n, 95, 97, 124, 125, 126, 129
Habersham, James, 12, 14, 16
Habersham, John, 56
Habersham, Joseph, 18, 22 n
Hall, Lyman, 13, 21, 22, 24, 31, 33 n, 41 n, 54
Handley, George, 41 n, 58, 62, 63
Head Rights, 14, 55
Head's Fort, 24
Higher law, 106
Hill, B. H., 110, 114, 116, 118, 149, 160
Home Rule, 133, 175, 192
Homestead, 48, 146, 157, 163, 171, 191
House, 36, 38, 40, 44, 45
Housing Authority, 182
Houstoun, John, 18, 19, 20 n, 21, 22, 24, 33 n, 41 n, 42 n, 54, 56
Houstoun, William, 58

Income tax, 124, 177
Indians, 14, 17 n, 56, 107
Institute of Public Affairs, 186
Internal commerce, 96
Interstate Commerce, 177
Irwin, Jared, 55, 62 n, 64 n, 77

Jackson, James, 55, 74, 78, 107, 108
Jacksonian democracy, 79
Jail cases, 90 n
Jeffersonians, 107
Jenkins, C. J., 110, 114, 129, 132, 143, 160
Johnson, H. V., 112, 114, 116, 117, 129, 135
Jones, George, 77, 78
Jones, James, 78
Jones, Noble, 16
Jones, Noble W., 18, 19, 20 n, 21, 22, 56, 75
Judicial review, 43 n, 70, 99, 106, 123
Judiciary, Constitution 1777, 42
Judiciary, Constitution 1789, 69
Judiciary, Constitution 1798, 84
Judiciary, 145, 164

# INDEX

Justices of the peace, 23 n, 38
Juvenile Courts, 174

Kent, 101
Know-Nothings, 110

Labor, 174, 184
Lamar, L. Q. C., 94
Langworthy, Edward, 30, 32, 56
Legal tender, 152
Legislature, Constitution 1777, 36
Legislature, Constitution 1789, 65
Legislature, Constitution 1798, 82-84
Lieutenant-Governor, 190
Liberty Hall, 17
Liberty Pole, 18, 21, 27
Limitation of jurisdiction, 44
Lincoln, 112, 117, 125 n
Litchfield Law School, 87 n
Lobbying, 164
Longstreet, A. B., 112
Lord Dartmouth, 23
Lotteries, 111
Lottery acts, 101
Louisville, 14, 74 n, 76, 95
Low Country, 14
Lumpkin Law School, 72 n
Lumpkin, Joseph, 98, 104, 105
Lumpkin, Wilson, 109

McIntosh, Lachlan, 49, 64
Manumission, 97 n
Matthews, George, 41 n, 50, 63, 73
Mechanics, 38
Mercer, 49, 72 n, 78
Merchants, 13
Merit System, 192
Midway, 11, 13, 24, 49
Milledgeville, 95, 108, 109, 110, 114 n, 118, 127, 153 n
Montgomery, 118

Nashville Convention, 110
Navigation Acts, 11
Negroes, 136, 148, 151, 171, 174, 179, 184, 185
New Deal 185
New Inverness, 11, 13
Nisbet, E. A., 99, 110, 112, 114, 116, 118
Non-jail cases, 90 n
Nullification, 108

Obligation of Contract, 74, 123, 155, 181
Ordinance of Secession, 115, 118, 120, 129, 143

Oyer and Terminer, 23 n

Parishes, 36
Patents, 47 n, 57
Pendleton, Nathaniel, 58
Personal rights, 100, 101, 106
Pierce, William, 58
Plural executive, 41, 47, 48, 68
Plural voting, 39
Police power, 92, 99, 103, 104, 169, 182
Poll tax, 191
Population, 11, 36, 51, 66
Populists, 184
Prohibition, 178
Property rights, 106
Protestant, 37
Provincial Congress, 20, 21, 22, 25, 29
Proxy, 38
Public Service Commission, 175

Quakers, 13, 14, 39, 49, 67

Radicals, 16, 17, 47
Railroads, 111, 130, 149, 162-163, 171, 174, 176, 180, 183
Recall, 85
Reforms, 144
Representation, 165
Repudiation of debts, 131
Rescinding Act, 74 n, 82, 86 n
Royal governor, 14-15
Rural electrification, 191
Rural housing, 191

St. John's parish, 12, 20, 21, 24
Salzburgers, 32
Savannah, 11, 12, 17, 18 n, 19, 20, 21, 22, 24, 26, 29, 30, 31 n, 32, 34, 35 n, 36, 49, 50, 51, 52, 72, 73, 92 n, 95, 96, 103, 104, 106, 114 n, 119, 150
Secretary of State, 170 n
Separation of powers, 35, 42, 65, 80, 106
Schovilites, 17 n
Single house, 35
Slavery, 110
Slaves, 13, 14, 23 n, 48, 49, 52, 73, 88-89, 92 n, 97, 99, 117, 154
Smith, Hoke, 185
Social legislation, 105, 182
Social Security, 191
Social status, 144, 153
Sons of Liberty, 18 n
Southern Rights Party, 110
Sovereignty, 105
Spalding, Thomas J., 77 n

Special jury, 43
Special pleading, 82
Special privilege, 164
Stamp Act, 11, 16
Stay Law, 152
Stephens, A. H., 109, 110, 112, 113, 114, 115, 117, 118, 119
Stephens, Linton, 112, 114, 117
Stokes, Anthony, 14, 40 n
Story, 101
Submission to people, 120
Substitutes, 125
Sunbury, 11, 13, 37
Superior Courts, 42, 53, 73, 85 n, 92 n, 105
Supreme Court, 42, 43, 93, 98, 106, 190

Talmadge, E., 188, 192
Tassels and Graves v. Georgia, 104 n
Taxation, 155, 169, 170, 176, 179, 182
Telfair, E., 20 n, 22 n, 41 n, 56, 62 n
Tidewater, 66 n, 67, 76
Titles, 39
Tondee's Tavern, 18, 19, 21, 22
Toombs, Robert, 109, 110, 112, 113, 114, 115, 117, 118, 159, 160, 162, 165, 166
Town Courts, 23 n
Trade Acts, 11
Treutlen, John Adam, 30, 32, 33 n, 41 n
Triors, 101

Troup, George, 107, 108

*Universal Intelligencer*, 26
Up-country, 14, 66 n, 67, 76, 81 n, 87 n, 132

Veterans, 174, 190
Veto, 40, 48, 68

Walton, George, 19, 22, 24, 31, 41 n, 42 n, 45 n, 50, 51, 53, 56, 58, 62 n, 64, 87 n
Warner, H., 94, 99, 114, 117, 153
Washington, George, 75 n
Watson, Tom, 184
Wayne, J. M., 94
Welfare, 157 n, 175, 182
Wereat, John, 50, 60, 63
Whigs, 109
White v. Hart, 154
White v. Knight, 43 n
Wills, 96, 97 n
Wilson, Woodrow, 185
Women, 146, 191
Worcester v. Georgia, 71 n, 104 n
Workmen's Compensation, 182

Yazoo Fraud, 73-75, 76, 81 n, 82, 86 n

Zoning, 174
Zubly, J. J., 22, 24 n, 37, 56